Atlas of Facial Expression

BY THE SAME AUTHOR

Atlas of Human Anatomy for the Artist, Oxford University Press, 1951.
Japanese translation published by Iwasaki Bijutsu-sha, Tokyo, 1980
First issued as an Oxford University Press paperback, 1982.

ATLAS

OF

FACIAL

EXPRESSION

An Account of Facial Expression

for Artists, Actors, and Writers

STEPHEN ROGERS PECK

NEW YORK   OXFORD
OXFORD UNIVERSITY PRESS
1987

Oxford University Press

Oxford   New York   Toronto
Delhi   Bombay   Calcutta   Madras   Karachi
Petaling Jaya   Singapore   Hong Kong   Tokyo
Nairobi   Dar es Salaam   Cape Town
Melbourne   Auckland

and associated companies in
Beirut   Berlin   Ibadan   Nicosia

Published by Oxford University Press, Inc.,
200 Madison Avenue, New York, New York 10016

Oxford is a registered trademark of Oxford University Press

Library of Congress Cataloging-in-Publication Data
Peck, Stephen Rogers, 1912–
Atlas of facial expression.
1. Emotions—Pictorial works.
2. Facial expression—Pictorial works.   I. Title.
BF591.P43   1986   152.4'2   86–12849
ISBN 0–19–504049–X

2 4 6 8 10 9 7 5 3 1

Printed in the United States of America
on acid-free paper

For Amy and Jared,
and Graham and Jonathan

PREFACE

The language of facial expression seems to be acquired without effort. Everyone uses it, and everyone understands it. Of all the human family, the actor, the artist, and the writer are probably its most vigilant observers and its most accurate recorders. Very little about facial expression escapes their notice—very little, that is, of what goes on at the surface. To probe for explanations, to ask why at every turn, is to unearth a multitude of surprises. Some of them are amusing. Others are startling. And still others may be annoying or offensive. In any case, discovering the true story of facial expression makes life more vivid. The drama of the human face is, after all, not just intelligible but captivating. For the actor, the artist, or the writer, gaining a full comprehension of this drama should be a practical aid in developing conviction and versatility of portrayal.

I feel it is of first importance for you, the reader, to be infused with the spirit of a given state of mind and feeling, as genuinely vivid as can be evoked and sustained throughout the brief reading. To this end, I resort to many devices and anecdotal excursions. But you must help. If the subject is Laughter, I want to keep you smiling. When it is Disgust, I want you to curl your upper lip! We cannot undertake this adventure dispassionately. It is for both of us to be steeped in emotion yet detached in observation.

The ingredients of an expression can be itemized as neatly as the recipe for a casserole. And the expression simulated can be as convincing as the casserole is tasty. But a recipe, as such, is inflexible, and its product is inevitable—like $2 + 2 = 4$. To appreciate the subtle nuances of an expression, one must understand what the expression is all about, how it came to be. Why, for instance, might you spread your face into a broad smile and chuckle if you had seen a portly gentleman on the street tipping his

PREFACE

toupee to a passing lady friend? Incongruous? Yes. But what has this to do with smiling and chuckling? Or why might you raise your eyebrows while trying to say the alphabet backward? Such questions as these will be the very core of the pages ahead.

An analysis of facial expressions cannot be undertaken without some analysis of the feelings that produce them. It is a dual pursuit. Yet this book purports to be neither a treatise on physiology nor a clinical study of emotion. It aims simply to bring into sharp focus those phenomena of structure or function, stimulus or response, that can dispel the shroud of mystery and reveal the true nature of facial expression.

In the course of your reading here, you will want to do much on-the-spot experimenting with your own face. After all, it is your participation that will make the adventure most rewarding. A mirror is a must. Keep a little looking-glass with this book, and may it reflect your growing understanding of facial expression.

St. Petersburg, Florida   S.R.P.
January 1986

CONTENTS

CONTENTS

Atlas of Facial Expression

CHAPTER ONE

FACT vs. FANTASY

The Mirror of the Soul

Try, if you have the courage, to imagine a worldwide plague of facial paralysis, where every face becomes a brittle, leathery mask. Your closest friends would be little better than walking taxidermy—a sickening thought. To break some glorious news to those you love and see no joyful light in their faces. To share with them the moments of your grief and be denied some visible token of their aching hearts. What a terrifying impact on human society if facial paralysis were to descend on us all! Fortunately, this is not a real threat. And so a dear friend can even say "I hate you" when you tell of some stroke of rare good fortune, because in the twinkling eyes and gracious smile you perceive what turns those words into a good-natured "Lucky you!"

It would seem that nature had deliberately planned the face to be the mirror of the soul, to flash messages for which one sometimes has no words. Indeed, it would seem that nature had endowed mankind with facial expression as an auxiliary means of communication. Yet this, most likely, is not the case at all. Many features of expression are actually serviceable. Some appear to be the relics of devices that were serviceable in a remote past. Other features are caused by physiological events taking place within the body.

Expressions, Real and Imagined

Certain facial patterns are standard equipment, common to all humanity and easily identified as the evidence of basic emotions. You will not find it difficult to conjure up the facial expression of merriment, grief, terror, or disgust. But many patterns are hybrid strains, as complex and subtle as an epicure's salad. And it's important to realize that a few so-called expressions do not exist at all. Following is a list of words that are often attached to facial expression. Some are actual and visible; others are the figments of lively imagination. Take a pencil right now and test your own discernment. Cross out whatever you consider has *no* identifiable expression in the face:

wisdom	reverence	sophistication
envy	guilt	mischief
respect	embarrassment	longing
malice	wonderment	jealousy
revenge	ignorance	innocence
apathy	hatred	worry
love	determination	bewilderment

At times, both fine literature and ordinary conversation take the liberty of attributing a facial expression to a person when, in fact, nothing exists but a knowledge of the circumstances and how he or she must feel.

Take *respect,* for example. It can be solemn respect as when a funeral procession passes, or pleased respect felt when a friend achieves distinction or acclaim. Respect is compatible with both solemnity and pleasure. But what shows on the face is either solemnity or pleasure. Respect is in the soul. One even speaks of respect for a dangerous animal. But this is taken to mean an awareness of the animal's nature and capabilities and an appropriate conduct that stems from that awareness. A respectful look is simply an appropriate look—one that is in harmony with the situation, whether it be grave or joyous. A disrepectful look would be in conflict with the situation. Neither grave nor joyous respect has a facial trademark of its own.

How often have you heard about the "guilty look"? Did you cross out *guilt* in the list? It is usually something about the eyes that causes one to speak of a guilty look. They may be uneasy eyes that lower and shift about because they cannot endure the searing gaze of the accuser. But eyes can lower and shift about in "not guilty" situations as well. To interpret the shifting, one must be familiar with the circumstances. A person often smiles when his or her guilt is detected. But the circumstances tell us this is an effort to appear lighthearted and unperturbed. In a number of ways, you can act nervously. And you can act nervously for a number of reasons. But wear a face of guilt? No. The Creator was considerate in this matter and put you on your honor instead.

Feelings of guilt may drive a fellow into motion, rather than stall him in a set attitude. The typical conduct is meaningless movement—the

fidgets. He quite suddenly feels an itching here and a prickling there; a lock of hair must be pushed back into place; the lobe of the ear must be pinched, or measured for thickness, or maybe just touched to make sure it's still there. He seems to be preoccupied with a sort of anatomical inventory. All he can exhibit, then, to betray his feeling of guilt is physical discomfort or uneasiness. And he does this by incessant changes of position or by senseless fussing with himself or things around him. On the other hand, meaningless movement is not exclusively the badge of guilt. More often it accompanies discomfort of other sorts. It is a common employment of anyone who is the object of attention, or anyone who is just plain bored. The mere fact that a person feels uneasy cannot mean he is guilty of wrongdoing! So guilt, like respect, is not itself an expression, but may be a motivator of expression. This is the case with at least two out of three of the words on our list.

The whole subject of expression is cluttered with imaginary faces. There is confusion about what can be objectively shown by the face and body and what is subjectively felt in the mind. Feelings come in a great range of colors and sizes. Most of the time they overlap to some extent. Now and then they shade imperceptibly from one to another and may do this within the span of a few seconds. As for the repertoire of the face, our concern here is the whole theater of facial patterns. And, now and again, strange things may be lurking in the wings.

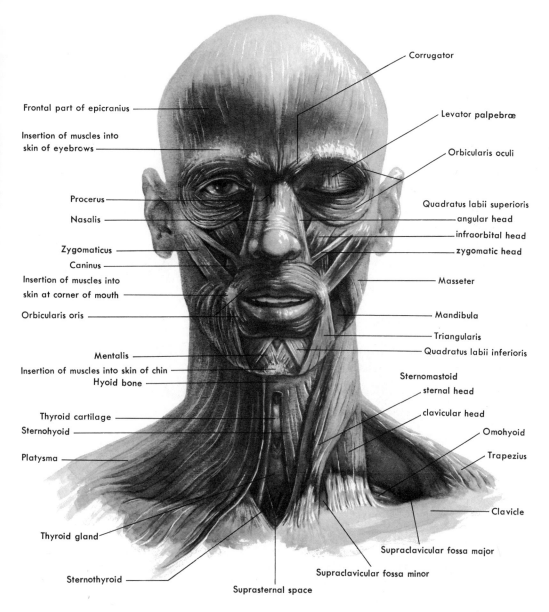

Corrugator

Frontal part of epicranius

Levator palpebræ

Insertion of muscles into
skin of eyebrows

Orbicularis oculi

Procerus

Quadratus labii superioris

Nasalis

angular head

infraorbital head

Zygomaticus

zygomatic head

Caninus

Insertion of muscles into
skin at corner of mouth

Masseter

Orbicularis oris

Mandibula

Triangularis

Quadratus labii inferioris

Mentalis

Insertion of muscles into skin of chin

Sternomastoid

Hyoid bone

sternal head

Thyroid cartilage

clavicular head

Sternohyoid

Omohyoid

Platysma

Trapezius

Thyroid gland

Clavicle

Supraclavicular fossa major

Sternothyroid

Supraclavicular fossa minor

Suprasternal space

Plate I Muscles of Head and Neck, Front View. (From Stephen Rogers Peck, *Atlas of Human Anatomy for the Artist,* New York: Oxford University Press, 1951.)

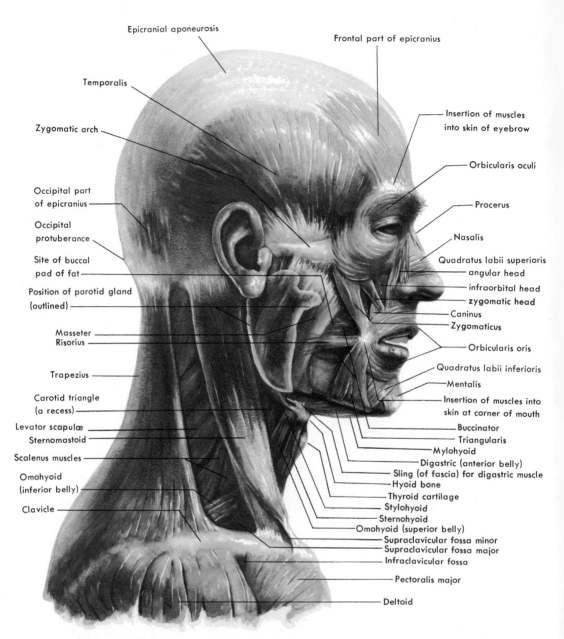

Epicranial aponeurosis

Frontal part of epicranius

Temporalis

Insertion of muscles
into skin of eyebrow

Zygomatic arch

Orbicularis oculi

Occipital part
of epicranius

Procerus

Occipital
protuberance

Nasalis

Site of buccal
pad of fat

Quadratus labii superioris
angular head
infraorbital head
zygomatic head

Position of parotid gland
(outlined)

Caninus
Zygomaticus

Masseter
Risorius

Orbicularis oris

Quadratus labii inferioris

Trapezius

Mentalis

Carotid triangle
(a recess)

Insertion of muscles into
skin at corner of mouth

Levator scapulæ
Sternomastoid

Buccinator

Scalenus muscles

Triangularis

Omohyoid
(inferior belly)

Mylohyoid
Digastric (anterior belly)
Sling (of fascia) for digastric muscle
Hyoid bone

Clavicle

Thyroid cartilage
Stylohyoid
Sternohyoid
Omohyoid (superior belly)
Supraclavicular fossa minor
Supraclavicular fossa major
Infraclavicular fossa

Pectoralis major

Deltoid

Plate II Muscles of Head and Neck, Side View. (From Stephen Rogers Peck, *Atlas of Human Anatomy for the Artist,* New York: Oxford University Press, 1951.)

CHAPTER TWO

YOUR FACE IS TRYING TO HELP

Nonexpressive Attitudes

Can you wrinkle up your nose at the bridge between your eyes? You can attempt this by raising the upper lip and showing your front teeth. Then lower the brows forcibly. Out of context, this contortion says nothing. It is merely grotesque. Probably you felt nothing in doing it except a willingness to oblige and a mild curiosity to find out what this is all about. But these feelings, if you had them, are in no way related to a wrinkled nose. Nevertheless, the wrinkling of your nose did signify something. Was it willingness to oblige? Or curiosity? Or was it simply that you're highly suggestible? This is the crucial point, and one about which we must be discerning from here on. Facial attitudes of any sort are significant. You "wear" them for a reason, and the reasons are sometimes remote and curious.

Much facial behavior is nonexpressive, yet it still serves a purpose. Every woman must have noticed her facial antics as she applies her make-up; every man will call to mind the comedy of his face while shaving. These are deliberate stretchings and puckerings that make the job easier or more effective. But such examples are obvious. In this chapter, let us consider the facial attitudes that may spring into being without relation to any state of mind.

Squinting

Squinting is probably the most basic of nonexpressive patterns. It serves to protect the most delicate, exposed part of the body—the eyes. Disc-shaped muscles around the eyes narrow the eye openings, while the

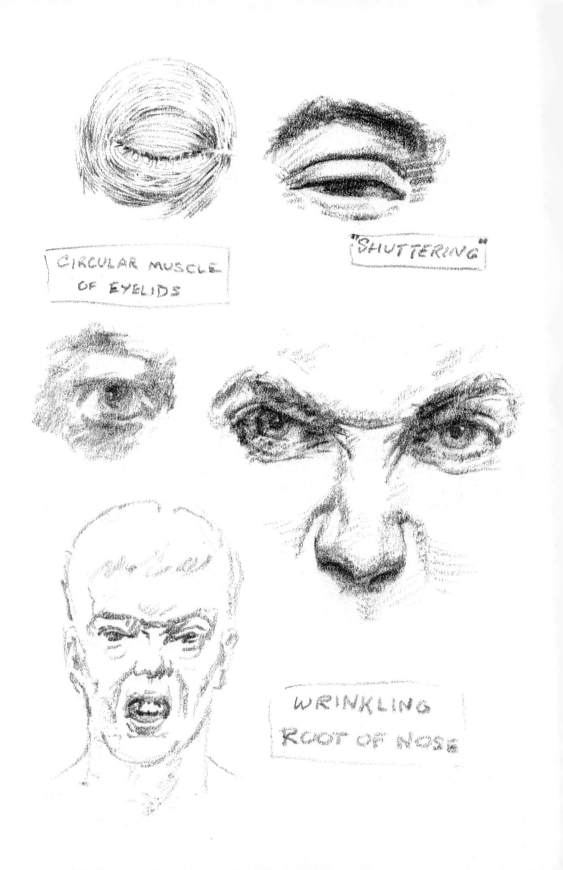

CIRCULAR MUSCLE
OF EYELIDS

"SHUTTERING"

WRINKLING
ROOT OF NOSE

mouth area may stay relaxed. In nearsighted people, this facial pattern becomes more or less habitual. You probably have certain acquaintances who just naturally squint most of the time. But ordinarily squinting suggests an element of temporary adaptation for the sake of proper vision.

Think of your eyelids as shutters at the window of a room. If a flood of sunlight is unpleasantly intense, you close the shutters partway to cut down the light. Of if a storm is blowing up, you might close the shutters tightly to keep out the wind, dust, or rain. Squinting is shuttering. It serves the useful purpose of shielding the eyes from harmful or unpleasant stimuli. Imagine that you have been sitting in a dark room long enough to have become thoroughly "dark-adapted." Suddenly, someone switches on a bright light. The sudden brightness is disagreeable. How does your face complain? Not only do the pupils of your eyes constrict to the size of a pinhead, but the circular muscle around each eye will also tighten, like the drawstring of a pouch. This eyelid muscle is actually elliptical in shape and might be likened to an old-fashioned oval rug, woven in a spiral. The muscles of both eyes serve to shield the eyes from above and below, by pulling the brows and cheeks toward each other. The effect is to reduce the field of illumination to which your eyes are exposed.

To consider a similar case of squinting, how do you look for the first minute in the morning when you have been suddenly aroused from a deep sleep? Again, the interference is the comparative brightness of light, although the morning may actually be overcast. Your eyes are just "sleep-adapted"! So perhaps in a stupor, you sit on the edge of your bed. Your face is serene with closed eyes; part of you it still slumbering, yet part of you is awake enough to struggle against slumber. You raise your lids just a fraction and discover that ordinary daylight is painfully brilliant. Then the light adaptation takes place, little by little. You open the "shutters" only a crack, then a little more. Before long, they are moderately wide open. And you can face your image in the mirror with nothing more serious than heavy eyelids.

It was noted that the mouth area may remain relaxed in squinting. There is no need for tension around the mouth. On the contrary, it is passively affected by what goes on around the eyes. You will want to consult your mirror to prove this. Can you discover what the mouth does? You will see, in fact, that it is impossible to squint forcibly without allowing the mouth to ride upward in a smiling curve. Some of the slender strands of muscle running to the corners of the mouth are anchored above in flesh around the eyelid muscles. So when eyelid muscles squeeze toward the centers of the eyes in drawstring fashion, they are obliged to draw these slender strands (and hence the mouth) upward with them.

REPERTOIRE OF
EYES AND BROWS

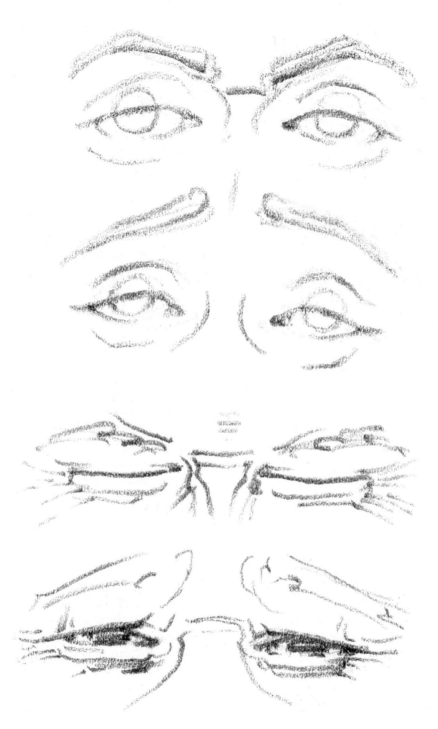

Grinning is, therefore, a common adjunct of forcible squinting. If the mouth is utterly limp, the lips will separate; the upper lip will ride still higher to expose the upper teeth. This might be the sort of grin you wear as you try to open the "shutters" to the morning light. So there is really nothing jubilant about the grin of someone who has just turned off the alarm clock!

During the day, your eyes are exposed more or less steadily to bright light. No longer does the sky blind you and cause you to bring a hand up to shield your eyes. It is something to gaze upon with pleasure. Your entire field of vision, in fact, is often a brilliant flood of light. At times, you are determined to pick out some small object in the far distance—to identify it, perhaps to watch it move. Once again, the shutters go to work. Squinting will decrease the field of vision. By eliminating distracting elements at the fringe of vision, squinting can thus improve the mental focus of attention. You may even catch yourself closing one eye completely while squinting with the other. Who knows? Perhaps you are squinting now at this page of print to blot out everything else around you.

Squinting is a pattern found so often at the race track, ball field, stadium, or theater—anywhere spectators must keep their eyes on a distant focal point of activity. It can become an habitual expression for some sailors whose life at sea surrounds them with only the great expanse of shifting water. There is not just the brilliance of the empty dome of sky but reflection from the water too. The desert or open stretch of sandy beach may offer similar problems of blinding glare. It can be cruel. The ever-popular solution is a pair of sunglasses. Squinting and sunglasses do not usually go together.

Among other things that occasionally interfere with proper vision is the weather itself. Whoever is caught in a teeming rain without hat or umbrella will seem to grin with fiendish glee at his or her own hatless and hapless plight. Or it may be the familiar "shower-bath" grin. The squint simply narrows the eyes against the spatter of the shower. It is common to speak of a "blinding rain" or "blinding snowstorm." A brisk wind will call for squinting too. When one is pacing into the teeth of the gale, eyes must be guarded from whirling dust. And just as surely, the eyes of bride and groom must squint against the bombardment of rice and confetti.

Such are the physical causes of squinting. The facial pattern is established at birth as a reflex for reasons that should now be perfectly apparent: protection of the light-sensitive retina within the eye and protection of the outer surface of the eyeball against irritating substances in the air.

You have noticed that you often squint when attempting to see distinctly an object at some distance. This is to reduce the overall illumination and blot out nearby distractions, so that undivided attention may be given to the object. At close range, however, squinting actually interferes with proper vision. The fringe of upper eyelashes gets in the way. Yet this is precisely what an artist wants when he squints at the object he is painting. The filtering out of extraneous detail leaves only the broad sweep of things. Squinting thus becomes associated with the act of appraisal or analysis. One may, from habit, summon up the squint when sizing up a person, idea, or situation. The employer, interviewing the job applicant, may squint by way of evaluation. The legislator may squint critically as he or she examines the proposed revision of tax laws. The architect may squint as he or she surveys the site for a new library. Squinting is an effort to sift and diminish—whether it's the amount of light or momentary distractions.

Try this yourself. First, with eyes wide open and looking straight ahead, note how much you can see around you, especially above and below eye level. Then squint forcibly, with head and eyes fixed in the same direction as before. You will readily observe that your field of vision is much reduced, something like fifty percent. It is not difficult to appreciate how this reduced vision is favorable to concentration of the mind.

Empathy

Up to this point, we have been talking about a nonexpressive attitude that serves a useful purpose. You may be surprised to find how much of your facial behavior is utterly pointless. There is a strange variety of compulsive attitudes that is mostly sheer nonsense. This unemotional activity of the face comes and goes throughout the day. But it will be more apparent in faces other than your own. If only you can be sufficiently vigilant to catch it on the wing, the procession of things you see will be almost comical. It is a family of attitudes related to effort, attitudes that would seem to be reinforcing an effort, ineffectual though they are. An interesting point here is that you will attempt to reinforce not only your own efforts but those of others as well. You are inclined to be generous with your face! In this matter of observing the efforts of others and reinforcing them, we may borrow a word from psychologists. It is *empathy*. It sounds like *sympathy* and means almost the same thing. But empathy can be felt in regard to inanimate objects, as well as our fellow human beings. We think of sympathy as a capacity for sharing the feelings of others. Empathy is a sensitivity to physical factors in a situation. You endow inanimate things with feelings and then proceed to share those feelings. The forlorn shell of an old house has careened jauntily from its original plumb. As we gaze up at the collapsing wreck, we too may feel giddy and wobbly!

Fun With Your Flexible Face

Flesh is not everywhere bound tightly to the underlying bone. Some parts glide about more freely than others. On the head, the most mobile region is the mouth. You can trace the line of its attachment to the skull. From right to left, stroke the gum above the arch of your upper teeth; then slide into the deep pocket of your left cheek. Return from left to right along the gum below the lower teeth. Complete the circuit in the pocket of your right cheek. While massaging the gums in this circle, notice how perfectly free from the bone is the lower part of your face. It is a sort of apron extending from nose to chin, and almost from ear to ear. No wonder it's your most versatile area! Brows and eyes are less mobile. Place your finger tips on your brows; then alternately push them up and pull them down. Can you feel the bony ridge over which they glide? If we disregard the rolling of the eyeball itself, there is only limited movement of the flesh around it. Once you have closed your eyelids and squeezed them shut, you have exhausted all the possibilities. As for the freedom of the nose, only slight activity is possible. You have already tried to wrinkle your nose at the bridge. All that is left is the faint dilation and contraction of nostrils. (In case you hadn't noticed, nostril activity is perfectly visible and under partial voluntary control.)

At the side of the head, many of us find we can tighten the flesh around our ears. This will make the ear lobe stand out from the head and will draw the rest of the ear backward against the head. Can you wiggle your ears? Such a movement no longer serves a purpose. Its very lack of purpose (at least in this age) makes it a bid for laughter.

Thus is the picture of comparative mobility. Already you can make your forecast that most instances of empathy will engage the mouth.

Examples of Empathy

You are now at a disadvantage, in case you wish to demonstrate your own acts of empathy. Forewarned is forearmed. And you may half-consciously try to prove you don't indulge in such tomfoolery. But the next time you thread a needle, take special note of what you do with your mouth. Most people will pucker the mouth, as if to help steer the point of thread into the needle's eye. And the next time you are wringing out a heavy wet towel, step before a mirror and watch the process. The squeezing will be

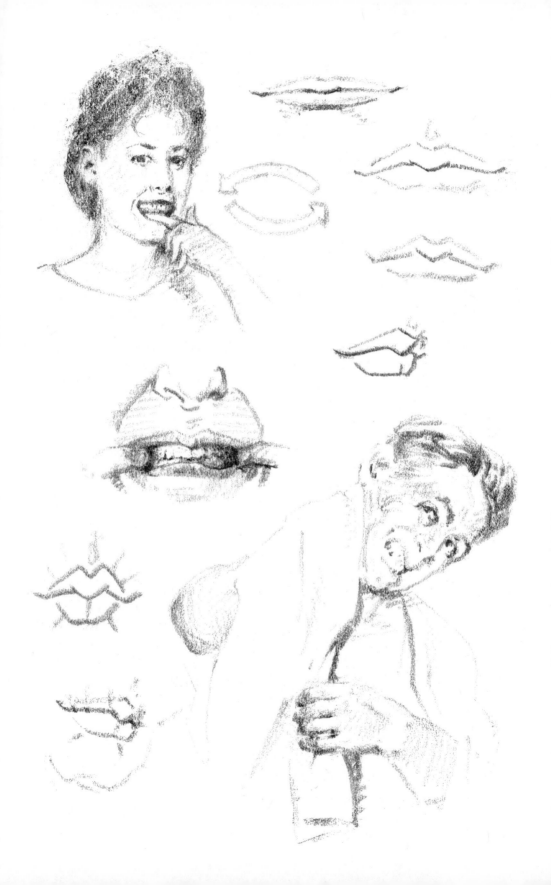

done not with your hands alone, but with your mouth as well. Actually, you will get a better performance watching other people. They will not be forewarned and will give you a spontaneous, bona fide exhibition. Consider the face of someone who is tying up a large, unwieldy bundle. As he strains to draw the cord very tightly, you can expect to see his mouth also drawn very tightly—the lips meeting on a line as taut as a piano wire!

At the arena, in the heat of championship bouts, feverish support is there at every turn. As contestants slug away, a synchronized mock battle is being fought from start to finish by the mouth muscles of frantic fans. There are, of course, the obvious attitudes that stem directly from excitement—from the savage bellows of anger to the shrieks of triumph. But the mock battle of mouths almost escapes detection, being slight and silent. Another type of performance is common at the circus. In part, the performance is high above us, where the aerialists defy death, gravity, and our own reeling heads. Yet, down below, another show is in progress: the sea of upward-protruding lips and chin, and even up-turned eyeballs and high-rising brows. What an army of helpers! All, presumably, to keep the performers from taking the dizzying plunge to a net or, far worse, the ground itself.

Now and then, one takes advantage of what is *in* the mouth. Try cutting some heavy cardboard with shears. You will do it, too, with clenching teeth, a silent crunch of molars with every crunch of shears. It is jaw muscles, spread out in the region of your temples, that bring molars together. Human jaws are like the jaws of any vise. When you or someone you are watching is crushing something you just cannot resist lending a jaw.

Of the other facial features that aim to reinforce an effort, only the eyebrows warrant a mention here. When they rise toward the hairline, they are being drawn by a thin sheet of muscle under the skin of the forehead. It should not surprise us, therefore, that any facial effort to make ourselves taller must be delegated to that forehead muscle. When it pulls tightly, it draws up the brows—and we feel taller. Stand two growing children back to back to compare their heights, and the contest is on. It is a contest to see who can lift his or her eyebrows higher! But consider this phenomenon from another angle. You yourself reach up to a high shelf, perhaps having to stand on tiptoe. And if this heavenward stretch is taxing your reserves, your eyebrows will come to your assistance and rise a little higher on the forehead. They are ineffectual in making you taller, but they have tried! Spectators at many athletic events are cooperative in this way. What a welcome lift they must give the pole vaulter and the high jumper! And it's all done with raised eyebrows. Accordingly, what a great demand on the eyebrow-raising muscles to witness the launching of a colossal rocket into space! In Chapter Eight we will have a closer look at brow raising.

At this point, it must be abundantly clear that our grimaces are not entirely the products of emotional feelings inside us. It might well be argued that facial attitudes are more often related to this business of reinforcing an effort than to the expression of feelings. Be that as it may, you have at least recognized the existence of nonexpressive attitudes. You are not really through with them. In the chapters to come, you will perhaps spy them in the crowd. But by that time they will be old friends.

CHAPTER THREE

LIVING DANGEROUSLY

The Trumpet of Displeasure

It all began in the nursery. You were hungry and wanted to be nursed. You were cold and wanted to be warm. You were wet and wanted to be dry. Something around you was tight, and you wanted it to be loosened. You wanted this and you wanted that. Your tiny body began instantly to have needs. But you were not entirely overlooked, even if your parents were not within view. There was yet another devoted parent: Mother Nature. She had seen to it that you were provided with a loud and disturbing signal of your discomfort. You had a mechanism in your throat, something like the siren on a fire engine. And lungs big enough to make the siren work! Even your own exhausted mother, in deepest slumber, could not be immune to such a signal. It was not exactly deafening, just exasperatingly shrill. And the household lost no time in getting to your side to make things right again.

Before many weeks had passed, you were making a valuable discovery. If you merely wanted attention or distraction, it was necessary only to sound the signal of distress. As if you possessed Aladdin's magic lamp, you summoned instantly to your crib all the attention you could handle. It became a device, and maybe you overworked it. Ceasing to be exclusively the signal of distress, it came to be relied on more and more as a trumpet of displeasure. You were bored with beads and wanted tinkling bells; bored with bells, you wanted blocks. Then back to the beads again. You were not always easy to please. And they must keep you contented at all costs. So the trumpet of displeasure became your most finished technique and most valued possession. It worked wonders—like Aladdin's lamp. Let's get up close and examine your magic signal.

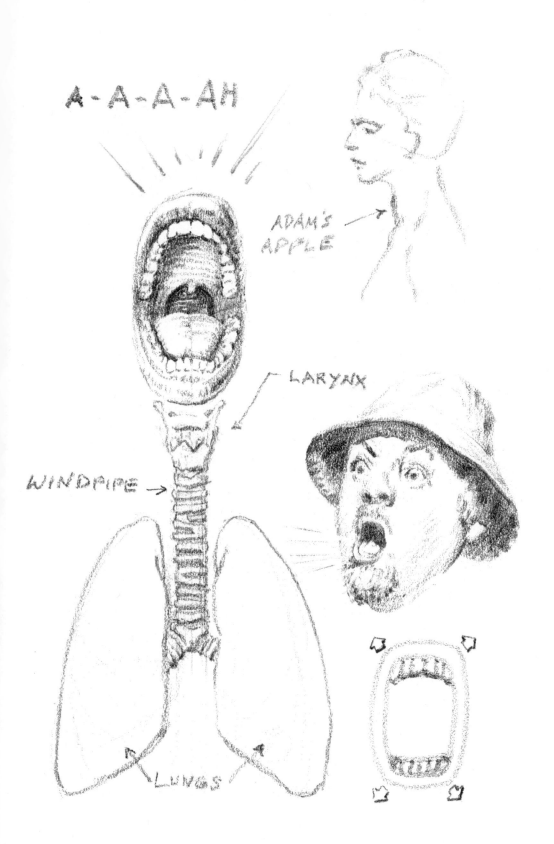

We might naturally expect the uttering of a loud and prolonged cry to require the widest possible gape of the mouth. So it is surprising that this is not true. A maximum opening of the mouth is generally accompanied by nothing more than "Ah-h-h." It's the face we make for doctors and dentists, people who want to have a good look inside. The mouth, when shaped for screaming out violently, is actually at less than maximum opening. A glance in the mirror will suggest how you cramp your larynx with an exaggerated opening of the mouth, and how you relieve it by diminishing the gesture a very little bit. (The larynx is your voice box and can be identified on the throat by a surface bump, popularly known as the Adam's apple.) When the mouth is opened as far as it will go, the rim has the shape of a tall ellipse, like an oval picture frame. If from this position you close the jaw just enough to make four corners and change that rim to a rectangle, you have made the shape best suited to getting out a maximum volume of sound. Here, as you have seen, voice production is more effective owing to the freedom of the larynx. Now all you need is lung power to rend the air with your spine-chilling scream.

The upper lip has been pulled upward, for reasons we shall soon discuss. And riding this upward wave, so to speak, is the lower end of the nose, especially the wings of the nose surrounding the nostrils. Back to the mirror, go from a relaxed face into a closed-mouth smile. Do it several times, and notice how naturally your lower lip is pulled upward by the rising upper lip. This is because the muscle fibers of both lips are knitted together at the corners of the mouth. What you have just demonstrated is a tendency that applies with equal force when the mouth is rather widely opened. Say "Ah-h-h," and before you have finished smile with your mouth open. This again draws the lower lip upward. But this outline would never do for a bona fide scream. The lower lip is too high and actually in the way. So, as if you had a hook at either corner, muscles pull the lower lip downward and make it protrude—rolling the inside outward. What you are trying to do with your lips is to outline the biggest possible square. One result of this outline is a full exposure of upper and lower teeth. (An infant's scream, of course, reveals only soft gums, or at most a dainty row of milk teeth at the center.)

This is only half the story, what is observed for making a successful blast on that siren in your throat. Now the other half must be told.

The Poor Eyeballs

Prepare yourself for astonishing news. The whole idea of screaming is to get the mouth into proper shape and then let go with the lung power.

Yet lower-face pattern is not as intricate as what you'll soon find in the upper face!

We can start with a hypothetical example. Suppose, instead of screaming, your object is to climb a ladder to the second-story window of a building. In your right mind, you would never simply place the ladder smack against the wall and begin climbing. That would be certain disaster. Ladders have to be leaned at an angle to the wall. The rule of thumb says the foot of the ladder should be out from the wall a distance equal to one-third the ladder's height. You probably learned the angle by simple observation, long before you ever attempted to climb a ladder. The very act of screaming (as you will presently see) likewise demands that you take certain precautionary measures beforehand. Failing to do so, you must suffer serious consequences. It is the precautionary measures that account for a complex pattern in the upper face during a scream.

Did you ever think of eyeballs as an out-pouching or outgrowth of the brain? In a way, eyeballs are a part of the brain—a part that is not safe within the bony shell of the cranium but exposed at the front to all the elements. You must feel sorry for eyeballs! They need constant protection. When you forcibly compress the air in your lungs at the top of a full inhalation, the great veins emptying into the heart get squeezed and their blood must back up. This pressure, in a roundabout way, is conducted to the eyeball, where minute veins become engorged. Vessels can take only so much pressure, and then they rupture. Obviously, this constitutes a hazard.

At the mention of minute veins in the eyeball, possibly you were thinking of those that are visible as scarlet threads on the white of the eye. These surface vessels do become engorged at times but the element of danger is not great. At times, we hear the eyes described as reddened, or less poetically as bloodshot. What do you associate with reddened eyes?

Reddened is used as a gentle adjective. Eyes are reddened with sorrow and prolonged weeping, or with the exhaustion of great anguish. *Red* is an abrupt word, almost harsh. It has no overtone of sympathy. One who is provoked to uncontrollable anger may show eyes that are red with fury. *Bloodshot* implies nothing more than a physical condition. It's easy to cultivate bloodshot eyes. Just limit your sleep to half the usual number of hours. Upon rising, make your way to a mirror and study the whites of your eyes. You'll probably decide it's more fitting to call them the pinks. We are apt to associate bloodshot eyes with lack of sleep, hence with overwork (or overplay!).

While redness of the eyes is something you can detect in a person ten

feet away, what most concerns us here is the possibility of pressure building up within the eyeball, within tiny veins that cannot be seen. At what times are you thus in danger? When exactly is the air in your lungs so compressed as to set up a chain of events that may produce serious engorgement of eyeball veins? A moment's thought will bring to mind familiar situations where your chest must squeeze in on your lungs with some degree of violence.

Violent Expiration

Screaming has been mentioned already. This brings a rush of air up from the lungs and blasts wide open a slit between the vocal cords which vibrate and produce a wailing cry. *Shouting* is only raising the voice. But, of course, greater volume requires a greater rush of air from the lungs. It may amount to verbalized screaming. When you *sneeze*, you draw a quick breath and send a sudden rush of air mostly through your nostrils. Whereas sneezing is a reflex behavior designed to clear the nose passages of particles so small you are unaware of them, *nose blowing* is a voluntary act for clearing the nose of troublesome mucus. Both require a rush of air from the lungs, but nose blowing need not (and should not) be violent. When you *cough*, you take a quick breath and hold it while squeezing inward with your chest to compress the air in your lungs. Then you let it escape suddenly under very great pressure, by way of the mouth. *Choking* results when the windpipe is threatened by stoppage. Usually a bit of food or drink went down the wrong way, entering the windpipe instead of the food passage. Air is sucked desperately into the lungs, vibrating the vocal cords as it goes past. Then a compression of the chest sends a return rush of air back through the windpipe in an effort to blast out the obstruction or irritating substance.

The examples of lung compression given above do not constitute a complete list. You will find some others in later chapters. Most of these activities are so commonplace as to occur almost daily, even several times a day. They are in no way unusual. So it is all the more perplexing to find that they must be considered as hazards to your eyeballs!

Eyelids to the Rescue

You get around the problem by wrapping something around the delicate eyeball as a protective covering and restraint. Internal blood-vessel pressure must be countered by some sort of external pressure.

Violent expiration is an event better appreciated if you think in terms

of a great explosion. An explosion in a building may blow out its windows because window glass is less secure than the wall itself. The weakest parts of the building are the first to go. The window is vulnerable because it is neither as strong as the wall nor a structural part of the wall. If a sheet of the same window glass were mounted, not in a window frame but snug against the wall of the building, the impact of an explosion would be less apt to shatter it. The combined strengths of wall and glass would be an asset.

Think of the eyeball as the window glass—in danger of being hurled outward by an inner explosion. This is not actually the case, but it may help you to get a picture of the eyeball's dire need for resistance out front. What serves to contain it and reinforce it would be the wall of the eyelids in a very squeezed-shut position. In this position, they double up in thickness and are not only thick but exceedingly tense. Here is the key to the pattern of behavior in the upper face during screaming. And it will be the pattern also in any situation where you forcibly compress air in the lungs. It seems logical to begin with the attitude of screaming only because that is what you, yourself, began with—and because it is the basis of so many facial expressions.

A Lesson in Screaming

Get out your mirror again and prepare to start screaming (silently!). All you have to do is combine the square-mouth outline with the squeezed-shut eyes. It's as simple as that. But there are two details you should take note of. If you will open your eyes just enough to peek, you will see a deep horizontal crease over the root of your nose, at the level of your upper eyelids. This is caused by the downward pull of forehead skin between the eyebrows. Less sharply defined is the series of vertical folds between the eyebrows. These folds are the result of drawing the inner ends of the eyebrows toward each other. Like quotation marks, they may be double (") or single ('). Such a brow pattern is called a scowl.

In general, the sensation you should have is twofold. Partly, you are trying to tug the eyebrows down over your eyes (a scowl), but you are also trying to make them meet and become one continuous eyebrow (a frown). The expression "beetle-browed" refers to the first idea and suggests the ominous overhang of lowered brows. The second idea is responsible for the expression "knitted brows," denoting the near union of their inner ends.

By this time, your brows are probably aching. What they have achieved in descending and drawing together is an exertion of pressure upon the eye from above. If you bring brow muscles into play without the contraction of other eye muscles, you have merely scowled or frowned. So now you must add to this the tightening of circular muscles that surround the eye openings. Surely you know what it feels like to wink forcibly with one eye. Do you notice how it draws the corresponding corner of the mouth upward into a lopsided smile? Now, wink with both eyes at the same time. This requires both corners of the mouth to be raised, so you'll have a grinning squint. Just like being in the shower, isn't it? Let your eyes peek out from the squint so you can see four or five short creases curving away from the outer corner of each eye. These are the familiar "crow's feet" wrinkles. Some people prefer to call them "laugh lines"! If your circular muscles are very tense, you can make out a wrinkle of the lower eyelids, extending from corner to corner, where your cheeks are pushing on the eyelids from below.

A while ago, we noted that raising the upper lip also meant raising the wings of the nose. This is a movement that facilitates the action of muscles lying over the bridge of the nose. When the eyebrows and the wings of the nose are drawn toward each other, they produce a special set of creases from the inner corner of the eye, radiating downward onto the bridge of the nose. Your eyes are never completely squeezed shut unless these "inner crow's feet" are showing. And only with all these contractions are the eyeballs adequately protected.

Now, to total up the ingredients of a screaming expression. For producing maximum volume of sound, the mouth is opened out into a square. To protect the eyeball from injurious consequences of compressing air in the lungs, all muscles around it are tightened. Brows are pulled toward each other and down over the bridge of the nose to make the "quotation mark" wrinkles; circular muscles around the eyes squeeze shut, producing "outer crow's feet"; and wings of the nose drawn toward lowered brows produce "inner crow's feet" on the bridge of the nose. This was the stage set for performing on your trumpet of displeasure. We have taken pains to get a clear picture of this stage set. And you must wonder why. After all, your screaming days are over. But it will be evident in other chapters of this book that a screaming face is one of your basic patents. It is the raw material from which many less violent expressions are made.

CHAPTER FOUR

CRYING AND PUNISHMENT

The Emblem of Trouble

For as long as you were a tiny, helpless infant, no one interfered with your wonderful trumpet of displeasure. In fact, those who took care of you depended on it. Meanwhile, your little body was growing strong. As the months passed by, you increased your range of movement and vision. The world around you began to expand. To a small extent you came to be on your own. So you explored. Now and then, exploring got you into trouble. You found that things on table tops could be moved, dropped, and broken. Sometimes they broke with a brilliant crackle. It was fun, except that someone usually appeared instantly to show signs of disapproval. What followed was stern approbation. But you hadn't yet learned what being bad meant. So your awkward little arm went reaching again. This time maybe it felt a stinging tap from that grownup hovering over you. The harsh tone of voice, the stinging tap, and reaching for things soon came to be a familiar and unpleasant association. You were being denied certain things you wanted. It was frustrating. It made you thoroughly unhappy. Then a glorious thought occurred to you: that magic signal! It had rarely failed in the past. So you tried it now, to summon help. But something went wrong. You had only further exasperated the grownup there beside you. There was no help; instead, more harsh words, perhaps more stinging taps. You had come face to face with your first shattering disappoinment: the signal was no longer magic. It could bring misery now as well as help.

More months rolled by. You discovered that in some respects life presents two ways of doing things: a good way and a bad way. By choosing the good way, you could avoid punishment. One good way to behave was not to scream out—even if you wanted awfully to do just that. Not screaming paid off. In a way, you were beginning to double-cross Mother Nature, who had so thoughtfully provided you with your screaming apparatus. But the facial behavior that went with it still moved into action silently. And sometimes it was to your advantage to show that you'd *like* to scream. The facial preparation for screaming seemed to have been instinctive; you just couldn't part with that much of the technique! And nobody minded, so long as you didn't rack their nerves with an audible cry.

The effort to refrain from crying out is seen as a deliberate effort to undo the screaming pattern. Since the inner ends of the brows were lowered, the center part of the forehead muscle must tug away to raise them. Try doing this with your mirror. Knit your brows close together down over your nose. Do you have that horizontal crease on your nose? You'll find it about where the nose piece of eyeglasses would lie. Now, keeping the outer ends of your brows tight, move only the inner ends upward as far as they'll go. In other words, try to make your eyebrows point to the center of your forehead. Look at the wrinkle design this makes at the center of your forehead. How is this different from the forehead over raised eyebrows? One notable distinction is the puckering of flesh at the center. And you will recognize the "quotation mark" wrinkles described in the last chapter. They are important in making squeezed-shut eyes. Above these are some horizontal forehead wrinkles, three or four of them, usually with the longest above and the shortest below. These "washboard" wrinkles tell of the effort to undo the pattern of squeezed-shut eyes. The washboard is bordered at either side by an oblique fold of skin. Here is an arrangement something like a TV antenna. This antenna pattern is the specific emblem of trouble. It is as good as if the wrinkles on your forehead spelled out an SOS.

Here, then, was a facial pattern that instantly announced to people that you were in trouble—without your grating on their nerves with loud screaming. It also allowed you to keep your eyes open and to be on the watch for a happy solution to your problem. This SOS formation often goes to work in spite of you. It appears and vanishes many times a day. All you need is to encounter some obstacle, even a mildly difficult train of thought. Then the SOS is flashed.

Recall

Where were you on the afternoon of Labor Day last year? How about two years ago? Three years ago? How far into the past must you dig before hitting a snag? Is your forehead puckering up in protest?

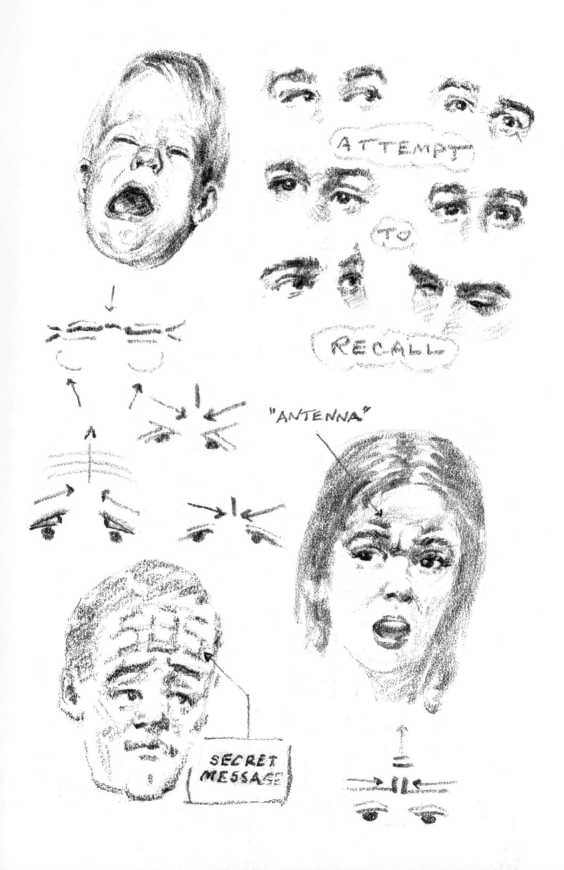

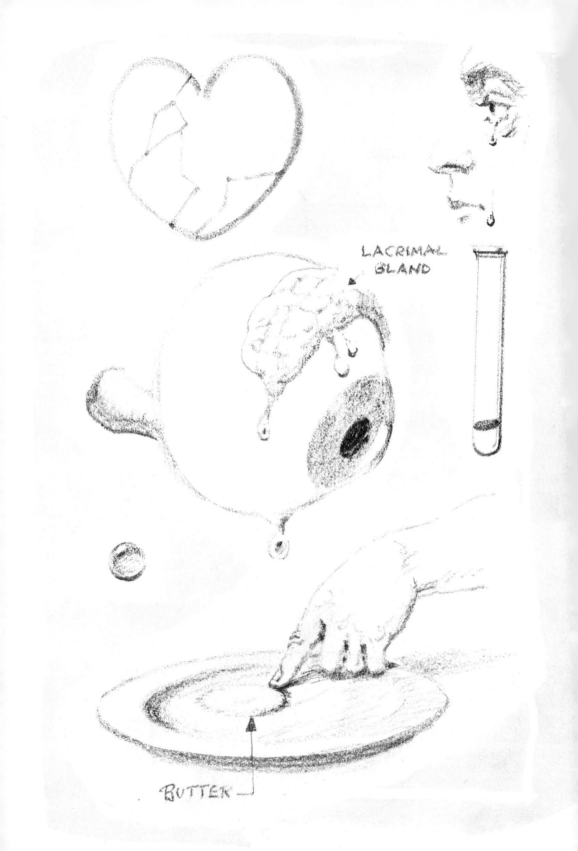

LACRIMAL
GLAND

BUTTER

What were the names of the three ships Columbus sailed on his first voyage to America? It's really not very important, is it? Yet it would be gratifying to be able to let those names slip from your tongue this minute. It would prove only that you remember what you have read.

Or try this: think of a word that rhymes with *film*. What about one rhyming with *month?* Or with *wasp?*

If the effort to recall is intense, your brows are probably drawn down close over your eyes. In part, this scowl diminishes your field of vision, shutting out distractions to promote more effective concentration (see Chapter Two). If, in your effort to recall, you are simply being a good sport and playing along with a trivial game, you will perhaps raise both eyebrows as high as you can. This is common behavior when the attempt to recall is engaged in lightly.

The response to a riddle, for instance, may be mildly serious. Thoughtfulness is provoked by the ambiguous wording and insufficient information, leaving the listener with wandering eyes and perhaps raised eyebrows, in search of a clue.

> The classic riddle of all times was the riddle of the Sphinx, and she devoured you if you couldn't guess the answer! But Œdipus guessed the right answer. Why don't you try?

> "What creature walks on four feet in the morning, on two feet at noon, and on three feet in the evening?" Take a minute to think about it. And think also about what your face is doing. Œdipus guessed correctly that the creature was man. A baby crawls on hands and feet, an adult walks upright, and an old man supports his steps with a cane.

Following are some exercises in recall. Take special note of what your eyes are doing. Probably they will be shifting rapidly and haphazardly from one thing to another in your surroundings. This is something like the fisherman casting his line hopefully into a number of places.

1. What made these words famous: "What hath God wrought"?
2. In the animal world, we call the youngster of a dog a *pup*. What is the youngster of a swan? The youngster of a kangaroo? The youngster of a whale?
3. In which of these disasters was there the greatest loss of life?
   Johnstown Flood of 1889
   Great Fire of Chicago in 1871
   Great Blizzard of Eastern U.S. in 1888
4. Which of these cities is farthest from the Equator?
   Tokyo   New York   Rome

Was your washboard forehead drawn into a puckered knot? This random, darting movement of the eyes, when brows are raised and the lower face is passive, readily suggests an effort to recall. The next time you must answer a question that requires thought, try to give the answer without shifting your eyes at all. The shifting is a silly habit, but you'll find it a difficult one to break.

Worry

Do you perceive any connection between an attempt to recall and the familiar face of worry? They are quite similar. In both you have the remnant of a physical impulse (submerged though it may be) to cry out for help. Both tell us you are in trouble. But they are not identical.

See if you can analyze the expression of worry and come up with its particular distinction. Just bear in mind that worry is far more disturbing than mere failure to recall useless or unimportant information. Worry has an eye on the course of important events in the future, often the ultimate outcome of a present situation. It must not be confused with fear. Worry is a feeling of uneasiness about the future. A person may worry about an impending examination or about the chances of success for a project, about the prognosis of someone's ailment or the prospects of getting a particular job. Some people take to nibbling their fingernails. Others bite their lower lips raw. Many are given to pacing the floor. But this is nothing more than general nervousness—a device for spending the surplus energy of anxiety. In effect, one is saying, "I shouldn't sit here idle. I ought to be *doing* something. So I'll bite my nails! Or chew on my lip! Or just keep moving!"

Your deportment betrays your feelings of anxiety more surely than any facial expression. But for now you must put aside this motion picture of worry and analyze only the arrangement of the face. In order to do this, you must *feel* worried. It may help now if you take a minute or two away from this book to worry about something. Consider, in your imagination, that very important appointment you made recently. And the time is only a few hours away. The weather forecast is for a violent windstorm. Perhaps your whole career hangs in the balance. Yet such weather could wreck all your plans. Think about it!

How does it feel to be sick with worry? Of course, your forehead is puckered at the center. What sensation do you have around your mouth? If you have truly simulated a feeling of worry, you must be aware of a faint downward pull at the corners of your mouth. If your response is still more evident, you are sticking out your lower lip. These are the leftovers of your pouting days. In this particular, the arrangement of worry is apt to differ from that of an attempt to recall.

Pouting

Pouting is the name given to a pattern of the mouth. It is the first stage of preparing to cry out. Before the jaw is opened and the lungs fill up with air, muscles at either side of the chin begin to draw the corners of the mouth downward. Unhappy people are sometimes described as "down at the mouth." And how about the phrase "long-faced"? Your face *feels* long when you are unhappy. At times, you just can't seem to prevent the corners of the mouth from sagging. And part of this preparation for screaming is the protruded lower lip. Look into the mirror and roll out your lower lip. What happens to the chin when you do this?

Your childhood was a period of conditioning. It was repeatedly impressed on you that screaming annoyed people. It had to go. So you compromised by giving up the sound effect while retaining just a trace of the facial pattern that accompanied it. The "antenna" became your token of trouble. The down-curved mouth was your badge of unhappiness. From childhood on, you could pout and pucker up your forehead to your heart's content!

Time for Decision

The next time you are riding on a bus or a train, look around at the other passengers. Some will be attentively gazing out the windows, and some will be engrossed in reading. But there are usually a few passengers who seem to be thoroughly unoccupied. They sit with clasped hands or folded arms. If you can manage to get a glimpse of some of these faces, you are almost sure to see the trouble pattern. Some faces may have temporarily frozen in this pattern. But more likely it will make only fleeting appearances. Somewhere in their chains of mental processes, they may hit a snag. Maybe they are trying to solve problems or make decisions. The mental obstruction of an unsolved problem or an unresolved dilemma is obvious.

All this may seem to imply that those passengers are doing a bit of heavy thinking. Probably it would be amusing to find how inconsequential their thoughts really are, just as it might amuse them to read your thoughts right now. On the other hand, these people may be lost in reverie. There is a difference between troubled minds and troubled hearts. So what, we might ask, is "heart trouble"? This whole new subject warrants a separate place in the next chapter.

CHAPTER FIVE

THE BROKEN HEART

Tears

What comes to your mind when you think of crying? A face wet with tears? Most of us use the words *cry* and *weep* interchangeably. But the original meaning of *cry* is still retained in certain idioms of speech. Some people cry out in joy, anger, or pain. Some cry for help or the view of a celebrated hero. Some just plain cry: "Long live the king!" "Speech!" "Down with air pollution!" The original idea of sounding off seems to be no more often implied than the shedding of tears. People speak of having a good cry, crying their hearts out, crying on a shoulder, and crying themselves to sleep. Only because you have good reason to associate the two ideas have you come to use the word *cry* to mean either one. The original difference is very simple: crying is audible; weeping is visible. From this point on, be careful to make the distinction. You have already had your fill on the subject of screaming (which is truly a superlative synonym for crying). It may be interesting now to investigate the nature of tears and the conditions that induce weeping.

First, what do you suppose a tear is made of? You've heard, of course, about salty tears. It's true that a tear is partly salt water. But there is about as much sugar in a tear as there is salt! And there are small amounts of potassium, ammonia, protein, and other ingredients. There's even an agent that helps to destroy some of the bacteria in the air and thus combat infection.

A tear gland hovers, like a threatening storm cloud, close above each eyeball. Its secretion moistens and irrigates the exposed part of the eye. Without continual soaking, the eyeball would dry out and become useless in a very few hours. Blinking of the eyelids helps to spread the tear secretion over the eye surface. There is a drainage system, too. The moisture

POUTING

LOWER LIP ALIGNED

LIP EVERTED

is collected at the inner corner of the eye, where there is a tiny pool of pink tissue. From here, the tears escape through an internal "drainpipe" that leads to the cavity of the nose. Hence the sniveling that accompanies weeping. An excess of tear secretion serves to flush out particles of dust, cinders, and the like. It is Mother Nature's own eyewash. Any irritation of the surface of the eye will cause excessive secretion and will bring tears to the eyes. Have you noticed the effect of a sharp, cold wind? On the streets, people heading into the wind may water at the eyes. They may even have tears streaming down their cheeks. You shed tears abundantly when peeling an onion because of the smarting vapor that rises to your eyes. Irritation calls for the flushing and soothing effect of weeping.

A simple experiment will help you to understand something about the way eyes fill with tears. Take a dab of grease with the tip of your finger. Lard, butter, or Vaseline will do. On a flat dish, draw a greasy circle of any size. Then pour water slowly into the circle and note that it comes to a stop at the grease line. Continue to pour, and the brimming water will eventually overflow its greasy banks. The circle functions as a container—up to a point. Now look into the mirror. You will detect an oiliness at the free margins of your eyelids, in other words, at the roots of your eyelashes. These oily rims have the same function. Not only do they keep the lids and eyelashes soft, but they serve also to contain the ordinary accumulation of tears and prevent them from spilling over onto the cheeks. Elimination is by way of the "drainpipe" to the nasal cavity. If tears reach flood proportions, they conquer the oily rims and trickle downward.

The tear glands will be pressed into reflex action when a pungent odor fills the nose. Nasal irritation is a sort of trigger which, by remote control, automatically causes the tear glands to discharge. The glands are pressed into action, but it is not certain that they are pressed into service. Possibly their internal drainage into the nose may alleviate the discomfort or reduce the harmful effects of the pungent odor. Or it may be an expedient, in view of the fact that any gas or vapor attacking the nose is likely, at the same instant, to attack the eyes. The fine points of physiology at work here do not concern us. Yet we observe that merely stirring the hairs inside the front of the nose may bring tears. This is a simple way to induce tears artificially.

How to Shed Tears

Have you a handkerchief ready? You may need it. Using something like a blunt toothpick, *very gently* stir the hairs inside your nostrils. Do this

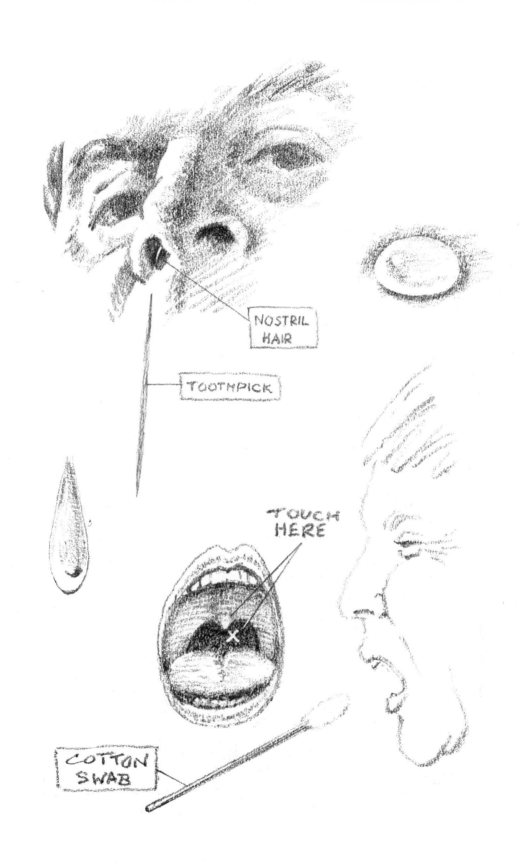

at your mirror. In a matter of seconds, your eyes will be swimming with tears.

With some people, a watering of the eyes follows immediately upon gulping down a strong alcoholic drink or a spoonful of very hot soup, or after too much hot seasoning in food. However, the burning is largely a matter of one's threshold of throat sensitivity. Some can tolerate hot food and beverages; others are burned and react by shedding tears. You can readily see that nose and throat passages are, to some extent, continuous. Both are sensitive. And irritation of either one may be the trigger that sets off a flow of tears.

If your throat is not especially sensitive to heat, and you still wish to prove by experiment that throat irritation will induce tears, try tickling your throat. If you are already adept at swabbing your own throat, you'll know what to expect. If not, watch out. The sensation is most unpleasant and leads to retching. Flatten your tongue with a tongue depressor, blunt table knife, or spoon. Then, with a cotton swab on a long stick, stir gently about the soft palate and behind it on the back of the throat. Be prepared to withdraw the swab quickly at the first sign of heaving. It may require a series of ticklings and gaggings before you notice that tears are filling your eyes. But, sooner or later, they will start. Tears induced by throat tickling are not usually as prompt or as profuse as those induced by nose-hair tickling. A more gentle method of producing tears requires no equipment whatsoever. Just indulge in four or five vigorous yawns. Repeated yawning is guaranteed to flood the eyes.

Perhaps you don't require such artificial techniques. Do you weep easily? You must build up, of course, the element of sad contemplation. For some, soft, sentimental music creates the necessary frame of mind if it is rich in association. For others, a visual stimulus will do—photographs or other keepsakes or souvenirs. And it might work to reread a favorite passage from some story of poignant tenderness. Still some of us just have to rely on toothpicks and cotton swabs!

Are you wondering, at this point, how some movie stars induce their tears? It's a fair question. After all, most of us would have difficulty producing a tear on demand. Yet one actress did exactly that for a nation-wide television show. At the urging of an interviewer on CBS's "Sixty Minutes," Melina Mercuri, the actress-turned-Minister-of-Culture in Greece, lowered her head for a moment of contemplation and then revealed to the camera her tearful eyes—in glistening close-up! Some actors may have to resort to drops of glycerine. Sometimes their eyes are sprayed with an atomizer that contains an irritating vapor such as menthol or camphor. However, some actors do weep genuinely because they have so utterly identified themselves with the characters they portray. They can feel profoundly what their characters feel. The great star of silent screen—Gloria Swanson—once told me that she always wept her own bitter tears whenever the character she played was overcome with grief. There were no atomizers, no glycerine droppers. Her only assistance on the set was a handful of musicians.

More about Tears

Have you ever seen a very young infant—say, a week old—shed tears? You've heard brand new babies scream, of course. But weren't they dry screams? An infant doesn't usually water at the eyes until he or she is past the first month. And, in most cases, tears are not copious enough to spill over the lids and run down the cheeks until the child is two, three, or four months old. Tears make their appearance gradually, and the date of the first overflow is quite variable. All this must suggest to you that you were not born to weep; it was a habit you picked up!

Recall our discussion of the poor little eyeball. When you got up your breath for a scream, the eyeball suffered distention of its internal blood vessels. To defend it outwardly against the inner pressure, you squeezed your eyelids shut. If this much occurs involuntarily, the pressure within the eyeball and that produced by the eyelids seem to affect the tear gland by reflex action. Either the reflex is not developed immediately at birth or the tear gland itself is not yet ready to function. Whatever the case may be, the reflex becomes established in due time. Thereafter, a firm connection holds between secretion of tears and any involuntary and forcible contraction of eye muscles. Tears may therefore accompany not only screaming but such violent involuntary acts as sneezing, coughing, and choking as well. Obviously, the tears serve no purpose. They appear only as the habitual accompaniment of violent expiration. And such tears have no connotation of sadness.

Have you ever heard someone say, "I laughed until the tears ran down my cheeks"? Or take a very ordinary occurrence—a yawn. It's not your first yawn that counts, but the third or fourth as the evening stretches on. Finally, your eyes water up. Try yawning a few times between here and the end of this paragraph. Imagine that you are looking up at a whole stadium full of sleepy, yawning people. One after another, the jaws open wide and stretch. You can't resist following suit. Notice that after your jaw opens wide and takes in a gulp of air, your chest slowly contracts to expel the air. Your eyes tend to squeeze almost shut at the top of the yawn. Soon enough you will discover in the mirror that moisture fills

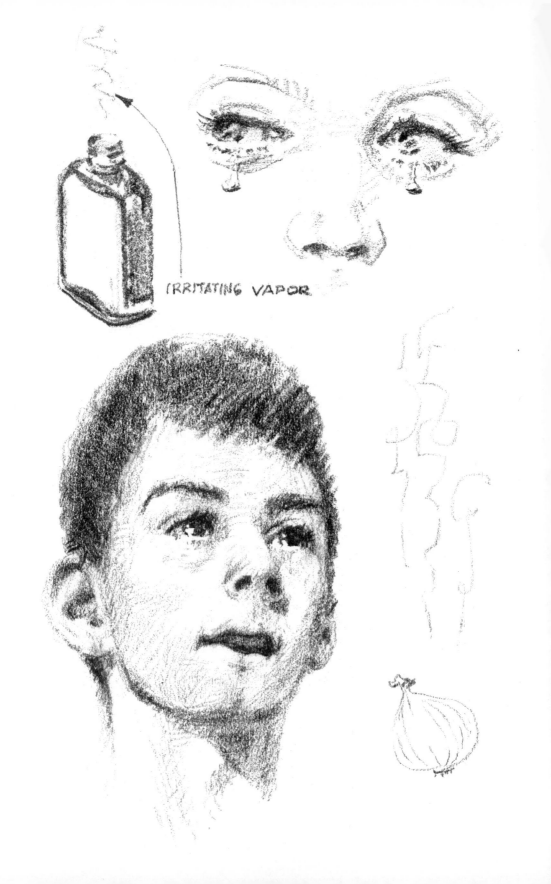

IRRITATING VAPOR

your eyes. There's more to say about yawning, but it's a risky subject here, when you are this far from the end of the book! We'll come back to it later.

Sadness

While you have been reading about things that may induce the shedding of tears, you must have noticed that the most dramatic and significant factor has not had more than a mention: the feelings of sadness. Tears are their very symbol. But we were talking about physical factors that stimulate the production of tears. Sadness comes from the heart.

Melancholy is a mood that almost defies description. It is a gentle kind of sadness, more to be felt than seen. Its particular feature is pensiveness, and pensiveness goes hand in hand with idleness, even if only momentary.

> The wanderer stops at the edge of the lake. It is sundown. Surrounding pastures and thickets are gathering themselves into the ever-lengthening shadows. Overhead, a meadowlark flaps its wings in lonely flight. There is an emptiness all about—an enchanted emptiness. For what seems to be a timeless pause—lifted from time itself—the wanderer surveys this quiet, sinking wilderness. Then it is gone. And he moves on.

Does that bit of imagery help you to feel melancholy? If you look off into an imagined distance, soberly and thoughtfully, your face will be something like what we might expect on the wanderer. It may appear to be a face in complete repose. Yet a melancholy person might feel just a hint of downward quivering at the corners of the mouth and tightening at the center of the forehead. If the melancholy is poignant, one's eyes are apt to well with tears. And these tears could be the precursor of an episode of crying.

William Cullen Bryant wrote a poem that induces melancholy thoughts—not poignant but austere. He called it "Thanatopsis," a meditation on death. Below are the closing lines. See if a reading of this tends to draw your eyebrows upward and toward each other.

> So live, that when thy summons comes to join
> The innumerable caravan, which moves
> To that mysterious realm, where each shall take
> His chamber in the silent halls of death,
> Thou go not, like the quarry-slave at night,
> Scourged to his dungeon, but, sustained and soothed
> By an unfaltering trust, approach thy grave
> Like one who wraps the drapery of his couch
> About him, and lies down to pleasant dreams.

When melancholy is austere, the eyes are usually dry. Melancholy is indeed a sadness, but at times it can be agreeable. This is the melancholy of reminiscence. And there is an indefinable sweetness about it. Scenes of the past are brought back in reverie. Precious moments are recaptured and relived, but now they are soft and filmy; harsh elements are sifted out. It is a revival of the good old days, the halcyon days, the way things used to be. Suppose our wanderer had come upon the quiet wilderness to be reminded unexpectedly of the carefree days of youth. Perhaps it was here that he discovered his first love or here that they finally parted. You might then have detected on the wanderer's face a trace of a smile beneath the tightened forehead. And if the reminiscence had stirred him deeply, his eyes might then have brimmed with tears.

> Tears, idle tears, I know not what they mean,
> Tears from the depth of some divine despair
> Rise in the heart, and gather to the eyes,
> In looking on the happy Autumn-fields,
> And thinking of the days that are no more.
> *Alfred, Lord Tennyson*

The general facade of *dejection* was described in the last chapter. The forehead is puckered into an "antenna" at the center, and the mouth is in some stage of a pout. Most instances of dejection are transitory. To-day's low spirits become tomorrow's history. With the next dawn, tomorrow becomes today, full of hidden opportunities and delights. This is the silver lining you count on so heavily. You can be dejected for hours, or it may run into days. You are dejected if you must slow your pace for a time because of some ailment. You might be dejected if a thunderstorm ruins your plans for a day at the beach. But such low spirits run themselves out in time.

Dejection is the troubled state resulting from failure, defeat, or frustration. If a person loses his grasp on reality and bears his fate out of all proportion to its importance, or if he simply abandons all hope, he will be rushing headlong into the wild state of *despair*. A desperate face does not exist. One who is utterly crushed by disappointments shows only grave unhappiness and trouble. It is all-pervading and all-absorbing. The mind, not the face, has become desperate.

Sorrow, on the other hand, is felt for the loss of something good or for having caused evil. If dejection is the unhappiness of denial regarding something you want, then sorrow is the unhappiness of losing what you already had and valued. But this is analyzing the cause of low spirits. In effect, both dejection and sorrow appear the same on the face. They come through in the elementary pattern of trouble: the puckered forehead and the pout.

Sobbing and Weeping

The facade of dejection may be preparatory to a screaming fit, or it may be the tail end of one. Pressure was put on you long ago to desist from crying aloud. You compromised by giving up the sound effects and hanging on to the stage set. As an adult, you get along in most situations without the sound effects. Only when your inner tension builds up to the breaking point do you falter and burst out crying. Even then, most adult crying sounds more like the sobbing of childhood.

A child's *sobbing* is the aftermath of a screaming fit. It is the wearing-off period. The child has finally suppressed further screaming, but respiratory muscles have not yet quieted down. The breath is inhaled in short, spasmodic gusts but is exhaled quietly. The sob is heard as air is sucked past the vocal cords on its way to the lungs. You can simulate this very easily. Just open your mouth loosely and expand your chest suddenly to suck in a stream of air *fast*. Do you hear your own sob?

Characteristic of an adult's *weeping*, when it breaks forth violently, is a convulsive shaking of the chest and shoulders. Most grown people, because of their long conditioning in the matter of suppressing a crying spell, associate some degree of shame with being observed in the act. One is usually impelled to cover one's wet face with a hand, to turn away from other people, and, if possible, to muffle any sound. Yet even this is often not enough concealment. The pathetic plight may be observed solely as a convulsive, rapid jouncing of the chest and shoulders. It is something like shrugging your shoulders. You can simulate this too, even though you don't feel like crying. Draw in a deep breath. Then tighten your chest to compress the air, letting it escape under pressure intermittently as a long series of staccato exhalations. The staccato sound of adult crying is the audible effort to break up a scream. Picture it as the scream of grief issuing forth not as a steady stream of sound but as the broken pieces. Does your experiment with simulated crying recall behavior at times when you have been utterly discouraged, outrageously offended, or hurt to the quick? Weren't you literally shaken with grief?

Grief and Anguish

Grief is an intense degree of mental suffering. It is not different from dejection or sorrow but is more penetrating and consuming. For this reason, you associate a violent crying spell not with sorrow but with grief. One is "burdened" with sorrow but "convulsed" with grief. And grief may stem from either source, dejection or sorrow. Sustained grief is

SOBBING

FORM OF BROW MUSCLE

FRUSTRATION

CORRUGATOR

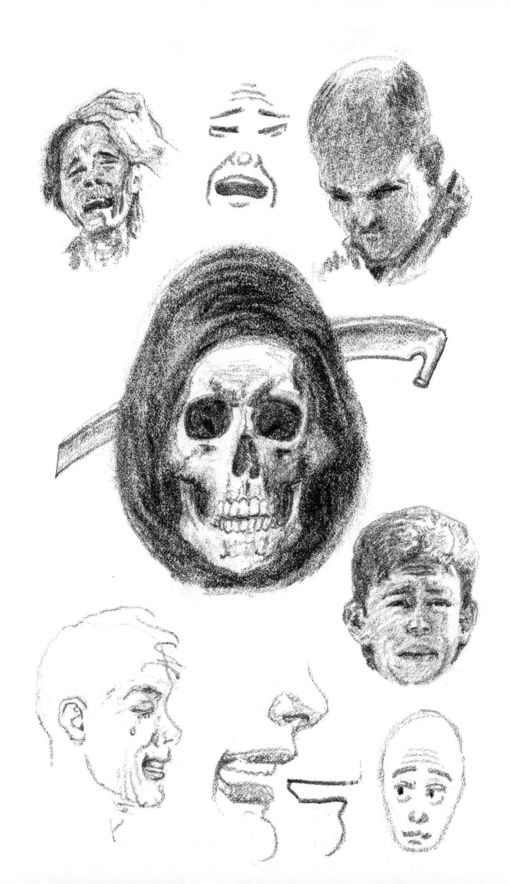

exhausting. It may even lead to prostration. Otherwise, it will subside into sorrow, which can be borne for a considerable time.

The face of grief will have the pattern of any troubled face. But being more intense than sorrow, grief breaks through the barrier of inhibition that was cultivated in childhood. It breaks through to the original screaming pattern. The mouth will be widely stretched to assume a four-cornered outline if there is sobbing. Otherwise, the mouth may be closed, either in the drooping curve of displeasure or tightly stretched out to suggest a grin. The latter implies a willful determination to contain oneself. The eyes will most likely be blurred with tears in any case.

It might be worth noting here that most of us do not collapse into a state of grief at the instant of hearing grievous news. Unless there have been forebodings to prepare one, first reactions to bad news range from mild surprise to shock (see Chapter Eight). One is gravely bewildered; that is all. The recipient of bad news is like one who, without warning, has been lashed with a whip. True grief may not set in for hours or days—until there comes a full realization of the significance and consequences of the event.

Anguish is a distress to be described as excruciating. It is mental suffering in the extreme and partakes of the symptoms of physical suffering. You will be given a close look at physical suffering further on in this book. For the present, you need only call to mind the familiar phrase "writhing in agony." Suffering is very largely a motion picture. It is a more acute stage of the uneasiness, the meaningless movement, discussed in Chapter One. Anguish is a greatly disturbed grief.

A person is stricken with grief who suffers great loss or painful self-accusation. A person labors with anguish when his mind is tortured to the breaking point. Anguish makes him frantic. If unrelenting, it may finally drive him crazy. This brings to mind such phrases as "gnashing of teeth" and "wringing of hands." No other emotional state comes so close to physical suffering.

To summarize the distinctions of grief and anguish, it might be said that grief goes limp while anguish remains taut. Anguish may concern itself with what has not yet come to pass. Grief has no such outlook; it dwells solely on what has gone by and can never come again.

Tenderness

One of the most noble of human capacities is that of sympathetic feelings for those who are struck with misfortune. These feelings are expressed to a large extent in one's gestures and general behavior, a manner of seri-

ous concern, and to some extent the inflections of the voice. There is often some trace of concern in the facial arrangement. Since you feel sympathy only if you identify yourself with the troubled person and face his situation with him, you are likely to adopt the trouble pattern you now know so well—the tightened center of the forehead. As long as this is present, the mouth may remain passive, turn slightly downward at the corners, or yet curve into a faint smile.

Sympathy is a fellow feeling with one who bears some affliction or grief. *Pity* is a feeling for another's distress and may imply that the sufferer is weak or defenseless. *Compassion* is a profound tenderness felt for the sufferer, especially if the misfortune is calamitous or inevitable. It is compassion that may smile tenderly upon the sufferer.

Common to all these feelings is the element of trouble, with its facial emblem of the puckered forehead. In your nobility as a sensitive human being lies the secret of sharing the misfortunes of your fellow creatures. Their troubles are your troubles. Nor do these fellow creatures need to come from real life. They and their trouble may be wholly fictitious. We identify ourselves with storybook characters to a remarkable degree. Testifying to this capacity for a sympathetic kind of sadness is the very copious sniveling and snuffling of a theater audience when the scene is a tender and gripping one.

So far, this book has dealt mostly with unpleasant feelings. Your mood must have been a sober one! But it's behind us now, the steepest and longest drop of the roller coaster. From now on, you'll be taking the curves in your stride. And some of them will be fun.

CHAPTER SIX

THE PRIVILEGE OF ABSURDITY

High Spirits

The adventure of facial expression began with shaping the face for a scream. It was an infant's equipment for unhappy situations. Then came the devices that accompany an effort to refrain from screaming. The growing child had to be socialized. And this was followed to its logical conclusion as standard equipment for the adult's unhappy situations. Now, turning our attention to the lighter side, a totally different explanation will be encountered.

Let us look back to your infancy once more. There were many times when you were screaming bloody murder because of some discomfort or need. Yet we must not ignore your contented moments. You had those too. How did the family know you were contented? Their ears told them. A blessed silence had descended. Or, if there were sounds, they were soft: sucking, cooing, and babbling. You were making little effort to inform anyone of your contentment. It just didn't seem necessary. How different this is from screaming. Contentment is a passive feeling. Even now, you don't really revel in contentment or ease of mind. Since contentment is passive, it has no facial pattern of its own. It just wears the face of repose.

As the mood brightens, so does the face. Eyes are well opened, keen and observing, but forehead and mouth may remain placid. Then, as the mood swells, there comes a *sparkle* in the eyes. It seems to be accounted for partly by a very slight filming with moisture but chiefly by the vessels of the eyeball swelling with the heightened circulation that attends a feeling of exhilaration. This must not be confused with the swelling of eyeball vessels encountered in violent expiration. There it was a sort of strangulation of veins. The return of blood to the heart was impeded; the veins became engorged. With pleasant spirits, the circulation everywhere gets a lift. There is nothing to impede the flow, but rather a fresh spurt to drive it. The vessels swell a bit and bring new life. There may even be a general flush of color. Considering that this means there is also a peppy shot in the eyeballs, it seems quite correct to describe these clear, happy eyes as animated or spirited. We behold in a happy face the signs of an alert and undisturbed mind.

Pleasure is passive, sometimes adorned with a smile. It is a feeling that's thoroughly agreeable. *Delight* is a high degree of pleasure, and more lively. Of course, there are intellectual and aesthetic delights. But they are of the mind. The outward expressions, if they exist at all, are apt to be of a dilute nature. An earnest and discriminating lover of art may study a canvas in some gallery with the most sober reflection. We may imagine he is picking it apart mercilessly. Yet an inquiry may elicit the fact that his absorption amounts to utter transport. He is carried away with aesthetic delight. Young children at play commonly laugh from sheer delight. Adults only smile. Their laughter must be provoked by specific ideas or events. Are you objecting here because you conjure up the picture of grown people at the beach, frolicking merrily in the breakers and screaming with pleasure? Look more closely. For each scream of laughter there is a laugh-provoking incident: a funny face, an ungainly attitude of the body, a mischievous prank, or the unexpected movement of the water.

Roguishness suggests behavior that is pleasantly and engagingly mischievous. An arch look is the facial expression of mischief, waggishness, and sportive trickery. The only distinctive feature of the arch look seems to be a tight sealing of the smiling lips, as if they had been glued together. This exaggerated effort at closure is evidence of the presumed struggle to keep a straight face and not betray the impish secret.

Gladness is radiant, apparent on the face as broad smiling and eyes that are clean and wide and brilliant. *Joy* is also a high degree of pleasure, but it has deeper roots than delight and may be even more demonstrative than gladness. Joy arises from contemplation of the pleasures of triumph and good fortune and general euphoria. Or it may be the prospect of possessing what is cherished or sought after.

The Principle of Antithesis

Now to dig once more into your past—this time for the story of smiles and laughter. The countenance of a screaming infant, you found, was

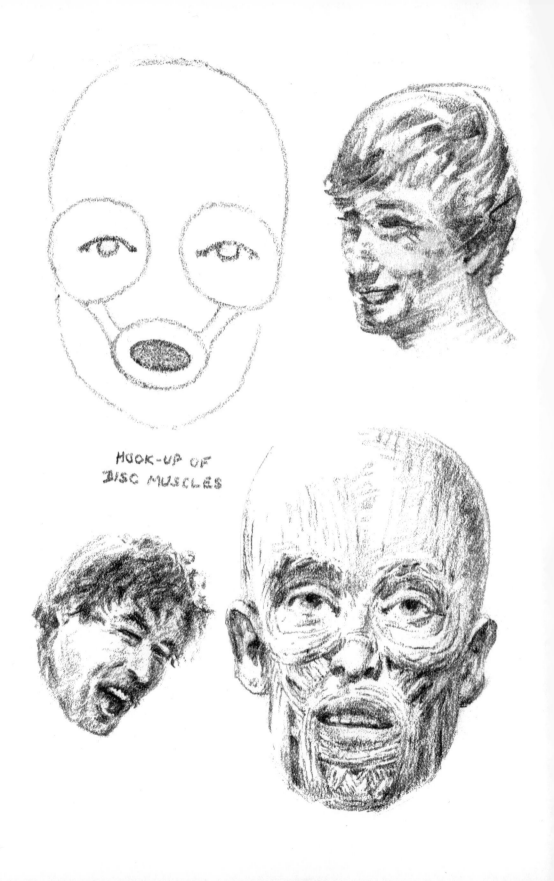

HOOK-UP OF
DISC MUSCLES

thoroughly utilitarian. Of what possible use is a smile or a laugh? Why not show pleasure by snarling instead of smiling, or growling instead of laughing? Why, exactly, do you smile and laugh? The great naturalist, Charles Darwin, offered an explanation on the basis of what he called the principle of antithesis.

When a dog is hostile, says Darwin, it stands stiffly with a straight back, its tail motionless and its ears turned forward. The dog is at attention and ready for battle. But when friendly, it adopts an elasticity that is quite the opposite. It lowers the forward part of its spine and wriggles, with tail wagging breezily and ears drawn back against its head. The stance of hostility in any creature is instinctive and utilitarian. Since it is the most suitable preparation for defense or attack, the stance necessarily varies from one animal species to another. A pattern of friendliness, according to Darwin, would seem to have evolved only as the deliberate and obvious reversal of whatever the hostile pattern may be. An example in human posture would be the straight spine, the squared shoulders, and high carriage of head in one who commands respect for his or her courage, strength, or ability. By way of antithesis, the stooped spine, the drooping shoulders, and the lowered head are interpreted as weak, helpless, or inferior.

The Darwinian principle of antithesis is quite generally accepted as an explanation of smiling and laughter. Yet there is a certain vagueness that one senses Darwin himself may have felt. Whereas he arrived at sound physiological explanations for practically every human expression—explanations that were based on the principle of "serviceable associated habits" or on the "direct action of the nervous system"—Darwin summoned still a third principle—antithesis—to account for the phenomena of smiles and laughter. The idea of antithesis is appealing. But it arouses some suspicion if only on the grounds that it allows at least one basic, spontaneous expression to evolve for no other reason than to express. Elsewhere, Darwin would seem to be averse to such an explanation.

The example of dog behavior in hostility and friendliness is a classic. Feeling hostility, the animal automatically adopts the attitude most natural and effective as a preliminary to attack or defense. Why, then, in friendliness does the animal adopt an attitude for display purposes only?

Very shortly, we shall see that the violent expiration of laughter serves as a release of nervous energy when one is in a pleasant frame of mind. The upturned mouth of laughter is, simply enough, an accommodation that allows the eyelids to squeeze shut more easily for the violent expiration (see Chapter Three). Facial muscles are not all independently anchored. A contraction of one is apt to pull on another. Contraction of the

circular muscles around the eyes is actually a mechanical assistance to smiling, because these muscles, in turn, pull on others that run downward to the corners of the mouth. The circular muscle narrows the eye, especially from below, where the lower lid is squeezed upward onto the eye. Curving the mouth into a smile makes it easier to squeeze the eyelids shut. We experimented with that in Chapter Two (squinting). And the contraction of eyelid muscles makes the "outer crow's feet" wrinkles. A hearty smile is usually crowned by a smooth forehead. Brows are lowered, the nose wrinkles between the eyes, and it is flanked by "inner crow's feet" (see Chapter Three). So if you consider it prudent strategy to smile heartily at your worst enemy, don't just hoist the corners of your mouth and show him your upper teeth. Give him the works! Forget your eyesight, and squeeze the eyelids together. And if you really want to fool him, draw the skin of your nose and the inner ends of your eyebrows toward each other. This will crease the top of your nose, and he has no choice but to conclude that you find him positively enchanting.

A smile is the preparation for laughter and may appear even though nervous energy may not rise to the explosive stage. Much of your smiling is willful, of course, cultivated and employed as a signal of warm feelings. Smiling at a friend and smiling at a joke would seem to be two quite different things. But the origin of what becomes a smile technique is still a mechanical preparation in anticipation of the release of energy.

If we concede that laughter does give vent to nervous energy, we must consider it to be serviceable in that respect, and we must look upon a smile as the only reasonable prearrangement of the face. The one question remaining concerns sound. Why does laughter have its own distinctive sound?

The Soundtrack of Laughter

Laughter is the audible feature of a frame of mind contrary to displeasure. It frequently has a contrary sound. Remember that a distressed scream is a wail issuing from a four-cornered mouth. To be effective, it must be not just loud but prolonged, like a siren. "HE – E – E – E – E – E – E – L – L – L – P!" On the other hand, a squeal of laughter has no need to be loud or prolonged. Laughter may sound surprisingly like a moan of pain or a shrill cry of distress. It may be almost silent. But its function is the release of nervous energy. The rapid contractions of the chest and the jouncing of the shoulders seem very similar to the convulsions of violent weeping described in Chapter Five.

It is, at times, quite impossible to discriminate between violent grief and hysterical laughter unless we are aware of the circumstances. News photos, for instance, can be very puzzling. Standing over the body of her fatally injured child, the mother may appear to be howling with laughter. Or the newly elected congressman, in wild celebration of his triumph, may seem to be enduring the most crushing agony. Sometimes we just have to read the captions.

Laughter is like a machine gun. Its characteristic tune is a series of reiterated bursts in quick succession from an open, up-curved, two-cornered mouth. So the voice produces a string of bleatings: "HA – HA – HA – HA – HA – HA – HA!" This staccato expiration is the very trademark of laughter. It requires an activity of chest muscles more strenuous than what is necessary for a cry of distress. Try this test silently:

1. Whisper the word *help* in a prolonged breath.
2. Whisper a chain of HA – HA – HA's in one breath of similar length.
3. Now decide which one would tire you sooner.

The next time you hear prolonged, uproarious laughter, take note of how the staccato cackling finally declines, graduating into exhausted groans and gasps.

There are many words that describe the sounds of laughter, and each one seems to suggest a different shade of feeling or quality of sound. In the left column below is a list of familiar types of laughter. On the right are characteristics that identify the types, but they are out of order. Match up each sound with its appropriate characteristic.

titter (snicker)	Loud, nasal laughter, often contemptuous
giggle	Horse laugh, coarse, boisterous
chuckle	Wild outcry of laughter
snort	Affected, silly, or nervous
chortle	Quiet, almost inaudible
cackle	High-pitched, hysterical
guffaw	Loud, continuous
howl (scream)	Hearty, continuous, exhausting
roar (bellow)	Sounding like a hen
shriek	Combined chuckle and snort
groan	One tries to stifle

Loud laughter is an act of violent expiration. If you laugh loudly or convulsively, your eyes will brim with tears. On occasions of long, uproarious laughter, as when watching the performance of a first-rate co-

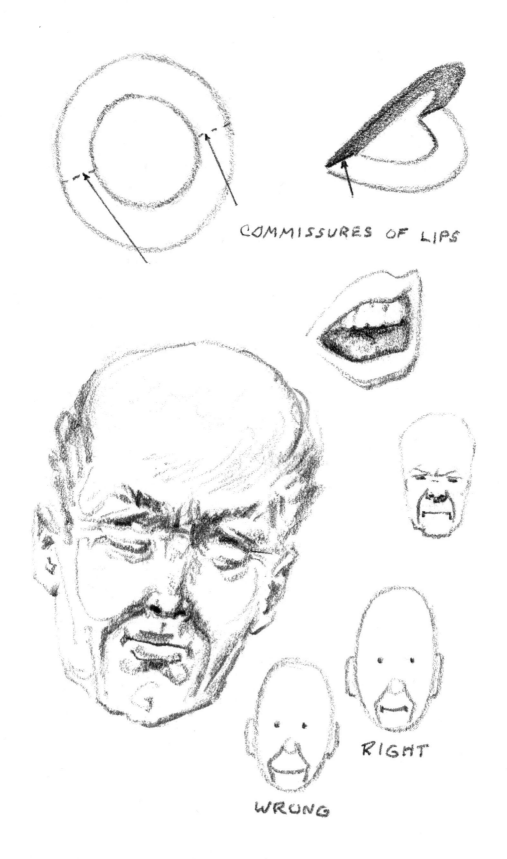

COMMISSURES OF LIPS

WRONG

RIGHT

median, tears will stream down over people's cheeks. The hysterical phase of laughter has been described in many ways. To say that you shake, rock, double up, split, pop, burst, or explode with laughter is to convey some idea of the extent of its convulsions. Milton, in "L'Allegro," speaks of "Laughter holding both his sides." In Shakespeare's *Twelfth Night*, you will find the now familiar phrase "laugh yourselves into stitches." And many of us have "laughed our heads off," or thought we would "die laughing." When one considers the rigors of violent expiration, such figures of speech do not seem amiss.

The Push Button of Laughter

Have you ever tried to figure out what makes something funny? A host of psychologists and philosophers have studied the concept of the ludicrous, the comical, the absurd, in an effort to answer the very ancient question of why we are amused. Not only is the matter very complex, but there seems to be no settled opinion. It is funny enough merely to think of scholarly people trying to discover what is funny! Yet, for our purpose here, certain elements do stand out. The English philosopher Thomas Hobbes wrote of "the privilege of absurdity." A moment's thought will lead us to the realization that man alone, of all the animals, can behave absurdly, and alone can perceive absurdity.

Laughter, like weeping, provides an escape for nervous energy. Either laughter or weeping may serve the tense winner of a beauty contest or the heir to an unexpected fortune. That laughter and weeping have a common denominator is evident in a fit of hysterics where uncontrolled laughter may alternate rapidly with weeping. Allow me to indulge briefly in allegory. Picture your life as a long roadway. The center part is gray, the neutral zone of Contentment. At one edge, the road shades off into black Despair. At the other, it shades into white Bliss. You trod along, filled with nervous energy, which is expended in the gray zone as work, conversation, thought, and so on. But you weave now and then from side to side, finding yourself on the darker side or the lighter side, still filled with nervous energy. If in either of those zones you trip on something that thwarts your progress momentarily, the energy under momentum in you bursts forth as sound and bodily convulsion. Your train of thought is derailed. In the darker zone, you may trip on a disheartening thought; then the energy is released as a weeping spell. In the lighter zone, you may trip on a ludicrous thought; then the energy is released as a fit of laughter.

The more nervous energy you have, the more violent will be the release—regardless of what trips you. For example, a self-conscious young

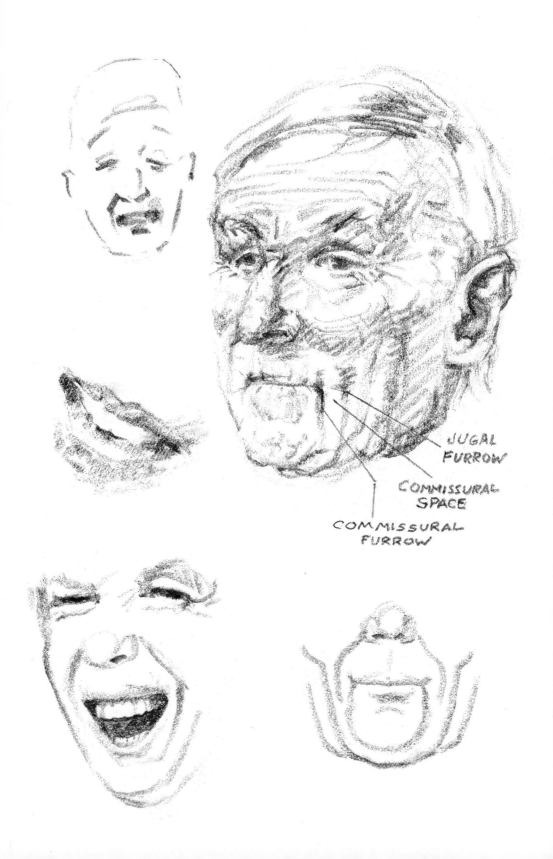

JUGAL
FURROW

COMMISSURAL
SPACE

COMMISSURAL
FURROW

man on a first date is apt to be oversupplied with nervous energy. He takes his date to some cozy restaurant, and they sit at their table looking over the menu. Suddenly, the young man bursts into uncontrollable laughter. The menu contains a few printer's errors. And the fellow has discovered items like "Prime Rob of Beef" and "Beery Pie." It is small excuse for convulsive laughter, but he is ready to explode anyway. He just tripped over a ludicrous idea. What we want to know is the connection between the ludicrous factor and a laugh. Sometimes, there is laughter where nothing ludicrous is apparent. This seems to be the nature of nervous laughter, laughing from embarrassment or surprise, and fatuous laughter.

Laughter does bear some resemblance to the explosion of a bomb. In the case of a bomb, the substance to be exploded must be chemically unstable, and there must be a detonator to set it off. With laughter, one must be pleasantly ready (unstable), and there must be a sudden and unexpected idea or incident (the detonator).

Tickling

It is interesting that tickling certain parts of the body should provoke laughter. Yet if one is in an unhappy frame of mind, tickling will only annoy or anger. So the first requisite of being tickled into laughter is, at least, a moderately happy frame of mind. (You are in the white zone of levity.) A second requisite is the element of surprise: you must not know the precise spot selected. (You trip unexpectedly.) This is why you can't tickle yourself. A third condition is that the touch must be light and feathery, in contrast to the firm contacts made with objects under ordinary circumstances. (The tripping doesn't hurt; it's inconsequential.) Fourth, tickling is more pronounced as the area of stimulation is reduced. A touch is effective with the finger tip, less so with the fist. (You trip but don't crash head on.)

You may have heard a person say that some thought or incident tickled him or her. It may shed light on the causes of general laughter if we keep in mind the essential features of body tickling. As you read what follows, think of these features as referring to the conditions required for amusement, or mind tickling, rather than for body tickling:

1. The individual's frame of mind must be a moderately happy one.

2. There must be some element of surprise, the novel, the unexpected.

3. The stimulus must be of a light and inconsequential nature.

4. The stimulus must be concentrated or focused.

The fourth feature in the list may not be immediately clear to you. With body tickling, it is obvious that the focus of a small touch is a more effective stimulus than a massive contact. In regard to mind tickling or amusement, remember that we are digging for the factors that ignite laughter, not smiling. We may smile throughout an entire comic performance, but only concentrated incidents will serve as detonators to the nervous energy of laughter. A joke brings chuckling or howling because of its punch line. And we chuckle or howl in proportion to how neatly the punch line is conceived and delivered. Were it not for the requirement of delivering a novel stimulus in a concentrated capsule, comedians would have little need for their gag writers.

Amusement

In the matter of body tickling, it may have occurred to you that the site chosen for stimulation must be a naturally ticklish area. The soles of the feet and the armpits are notoriously ticklish. The ribs are also very sensitive to tickling. On the other hand, some parts of the body do not tickle easily. Perhaps we can look for a parallel in mind tickling. Can it be that only certain areas of our perception and thinking will respond to a stimulus by what we call being amused? This would seem to be the case. Whereas the elements of surprise, levity, and small focus have to do with delivering the touch, there is no tickling unless the touch is on a naturally vulnerable spot. It would appear that what is naturally ticklish in our minds is the perception and recognition of what is contrary to the status quo of situations and human conduct. An obvious example would be the pugilist who is suddenly revealed as the winner of a poetry contest.

A more enchanting example is the sort of situation that, by contrast, bestows a feeling of sudden glory or exalted superiority. Let us say that someone inadvertently betrays ignorance of a point that is familiar to you. Mrs. Malaprop was a character in Sheridan's *The Rivals* who was noted for her word blunders: "Everybody's conjugating at the other end of the hall." A few years ago, there was a television interview with the nation's foremost fashion model. Her appearance was that of a saucy and voluptuous tigress. When asked, "Miss Gorgeous, to what do you attribute your phenomenal success as a model?" she replied, "I guess you'd call it my great *dearth* of experience." You are amused by "malaprops" because they inflate the sense of your own sophistication.

Perhaps even more common in your experience is the feeling of sudden glory when you stumble onto an error in print—the typo. This is error indeed, but nothing more. Yet, knowing this, you find a molecule of pleasure in being sufficiently sharp-eyed and educoted to catch amis take.

SMILING
TO
LAUGHTER

In the following list, the lefthand column has to do with things as they usually are or should be, the status quo. A look at the righthand column will call to mind the sort of contrary subject matter that is naturally vulnerable as a detonator of laughter.

Status quo (invulnerable)	*Contrary to status quo (vulnerable)*
order, composure	disorder, derangement, confusion
naturalness, usualness	unnaturalness, unusualness, oddity, strangeness, grotesqueness
dignity, decorum	indignity, dignity disrobed, vulgarity
gracefulness, suavity	awkwardness, clumsiness, bungling
seriousness, earnestness	ridiculousness, frivolity, foolishness
common sense, credibility	absurdity, preposterousness
congruity, fitness, suitability, appropriateness, harmony	incongruity, unfitness, unsuitability, inappropriateness, disharmony
effectiveness, potency, strength	ineffectiveness, impotence, weakness
knowledge, information, wisdom, sophistication	ignorance, stupidity, naiveté
experience, mastery, skill	inexperience, neophytism, beginnership
virtue, righteousness	vice, wrongdoing, crime
propriety, decency	impropriety, indecency, boorishness
generosity	stinginess
frugality	prodigality

In using the word *ludicrous*, we are designating contrariness to the status quo. What is acceptable in one culture may be ludicrous in another. Exactly what is ludicrous is determined by the set of the mind. We don't laugh at something solely because it is ludicrous by our standards. Recall the classic scene where Charlie Chaplin, with napkin under chin, feasts with absurd decorum on a boiled shoe. But probably you are not laughing at the ludicrous image in your mind. As you have already noted, there will be a release of nervous energy only when the energy is arrested by your tripping on an idea. In a pleasant frame of mind, you must have perceived its lighter side in order to be tripped into laughter instead of a crying spell. And the tripping must be brought about by some small, unexpected, or novel particular that is contrary to your sense of status quo.

The Laugh Test

As you read along here, try to pinpoint where you laugh and why.

> An Irishman at a wake drank all evening until he passed out. Hours later, he wakened to find himself lying in a coffin. Said he,

"If I'm still alive, what am I doing in this coffin? But if I'm dead, then how come I have to go to the toilet?"

The incongruity is made amusing by the order of the conditional clauses. The vulgarism about a need to relieve himself is saved for the punch line—always at the end.

A friend tells me this story about a formal dinner he attended. The buffet-style table was arranged elegantly with plates of sumptuous delicacies. As he waited his turn, the diamond-studded matron ahead of him was about to serve herself from the tender, young stems of asparagus lying side by side on a silver platter. To my friend's consternation, she picked up a long carving knife and proceeded to slice off all the asparagus tips and scoop them onto her plate. Turning to my friend, who had gasped in astonishment, she remarked, "Oh, didn't you know? This is the best part of the asparagus!"

This one is short and to the point:

Two cannibals were relaxing after dinner. "Your wife," said one, "makes a wonderful pot roast." "Yes," replied the other. "And I'm certainly going to miss her."

The Twist

The unexpected turn is called the twist. A pun is a very basic twist that results from a play on words. We find a good example in the following quaint rhyme of Tom Hood:

Ben Battle was a soldier bold and used to war's alarms.
A cannon ball took off his legs, so he laid down his arms.

Whether in words or events, the twist is a basic ingredient of fun. Repeated twists are so apparent in the peek-a-boo game that adults play with infants. As long as the game goes along in a frivolous spirit, the infant never fails to find it amusing. And he lets you know it with his clucking and gurgling sounds. Later, through childhood, there will be similar types of amusement on a higher plane. The magician will bring forth bouquets and silken flags from nowhere; in a puff of smoke, these are transformed into fluttering birds. And then they disappear altogether, while the children laugh gleefully. As we grow older, our own struggles to be well-mannered, righteous, and dignified may cause us to take a perverse pleasure in seeing another's dignity undressed. It's the pretentious clown whose beguiling wiles lead him to the inevitable banana-skin skid.

Human Foibles

Humor born of human foibles cannot be outdated. Absent-mindedness, for one, will continue to nourish humor because it will continue to nourish absurdity. Take the case of Aunt Minnie. She was notoriously absent-minded but just as notoriously spilling over with good intentions. One day in midsummer when ominous storm clouds hung low in the sky, a caller was about to depart. No sooner had the caller left the house than the sky opened up to let the rain come down in buckets. Aunt Minnie quickly found an umbrella, opened it, and chased after her friend to offer it. But the well-raincoated friend smiled as she asked how Aunt Minnie expected to get back to the house dry. In any case, the friend had only a short distance to go and declined the offer. Aunt Minnie, seeing that her mission was unsuccessful, closed the umbrella reluctantly and hurried back to the house—soaked to the skin!

If such anecdotes provoke amusement, it is because they are light and told without malice, and because they have a ridiculous and unexpected turn.

In conclusion, there is one variety of humor that is an extravagant brand of the ridiculous. It expands to the proportions of a satirical caricature. With impertinence, it would be a mockery—like Chaplin's film *The Double-Cross*. Being kindly, it can be called a travesty or a burlesque. Such is the Chaplin film satire on *Modern Times*. Many of Chaplin's films are remarkably skillful blends of quixotic humor and pathos. We are on the verge of tears but burst out laughing. We seem to be commiserating under our breath, "You pathetic little fellow! You try so desperately hard to be kind and lofty and heroic—and somehow you always botch it up!"

CHAPTER SEVEN

A MATTER
OF GENDER

The Awakening

As a growing child, your life began to unfold and shape itself rather like a long gallery with many doors. Every door opened onto some new quarter of experience in store for you. One of the early discoveries was gravity. It pulled on your toys, your upset glass of milk, even on you. Everything, it seemed, would drop to the ground if you let go—except the bright-colored gas balloons. Years later, perhaps, you were enrolled in a chemistry class and learned that balloons can be inflated with hydrogen, a gas even lighter than air. It became clear then why some balloons could escape to the sky. If you continued to study, possibly you opened still another door, this one to a simplified cosmology. It may have stirred in your mind thoughts of your childhood balloon and how its hydrogen ultimately escaped from the Earth's atmosphere and went to join its fellow atoms, scattered through a void that you could not hope to visualize without even more years of learning and contemplation. Every now and then, another door appeared in the gallery of your life, and a new field of experience was discovered.

One particular door opened slowly in your early teens, a little at a time. What you found there could scarcely be set down in words. It was a mysterious force, unlike any other quarter of experience. And once it was opened, you could never close that door. The strange new force was released, and it crept into your very being to lodge there for the rest of your life. And with it came to be implanted the sensitivity to a complementary force in others, generally of the opposite sex. It was a force that would enable you to swing open the great doors of adult love—the most universally treasured of all experiences.

LOVE - SICK ?

Stardust

Physical attraction, you found, was a highly speculative matter. You were drawn, as by a magnet, toward one particular person. It was sheer luck if that person were also drawn toward you in particular. It was strictly a game of chance. Having the prize in view, it was in order now to thicken the plot deliberately by efforts to make yourself as appealing as possible. You behaved in such a way that the focus of attention was on your gold-star points. You were playing the role of what you'd like to be. And you hoped, quite naturally, that any defects would go unnoticed. You wished to appear as a debonair, healthy, and gracious individual, with ambitions and abilities. For a while, this would be enough. Any problems that beset you would be more sympathetically received later on. For the present, all must be sweetness and light.

When you and your loved one discovered that you shared equally a pleasure in each other's company, the relationship may have expanded into the full bloom of love and courtship. At this point, both of you probably felt you were made for each other, so perfect was the combination. Each face glowed with *adoration* for the other, and this is the most reverential kind of esteem—some degree of smile, crowned with the gaze of widely opened eyes. The rest of the world was excluded from this segment of your life. No longer were you a complete person, because there was that "other half" that now must be near to make you complete. In fact, every hour of absence from the loved one was almost intolerably dreary. Your frequent low spirits at such times caused others to wonder what ailed you.

But there was another reason for the low spirits. This new-found attachment was so exhilarating and so glorious that the slightest disharmony seemed, by contrast, to loom into unreasonable proportions. Both you and the loved one had become hypersensitive—not only in respect to each other but toward everyone and everything. The trashiest verse might hold for you some special secret meaning. A current hit song might have a special grip on you, simply because the lyrics said what was in your own heart. Where yesterday's sunset was merely the setting of the sun, today's was a thing of devastating beauty—ephemeral, exciting, majestic. It was little wonder that you were touchy about small blemishes in this ecstatic period. Your loved one could hurt you so easily. Sometimes, the most casual social encounters of that loved one became suspect. Misunderstandings slipped in like houseflies. And there were the broodings that go with being hurt or misunderstood. Appetites had a notorious way of evaporating at mealtime. And just as notorious was the fitful struggle to sleep at night. Truly, being in love can be far from pure bliss. Nor is the face of the lover always a truly happy one. Much of the time he or she looks just plain sick!

Romantic Love

Romantic love has been defined as love plus frustration. It's the perpetual and inevitable encountering of obstacles that sustains the intensity of romantic love. Once these obstacles are escaped or conquered, the volatile romance of flowers and fiddle strings must become a memory.

The face of romantic love is not unique. At times, it may be a sick, unhappy face. At other times, it is happy—full of brightness and flushed with animation. In Chapter Six we mentioned sparkle in the eyes and attributed it partly to the quickened circulation of blood that attends any feeling of exhilaration. Eyes then are bright and animated, having the clean look that comes partly from a laundry-soap whiteness of the eyeball. Here are the limpid, starry eyes of young people in love. The countenance of love is usually soft and gentle in the presence of the loved one. Yet it may oscillate confusingly between joy and downright sickness. In this hypersensitive phase, lovers' eyes may well with tears at the slightest provocation. These are the tears of *tender joy*—a joy that must have its complement of sadness. So we hear that "parting is such sweet sorrow." The farewell of lovers is an incongruous mixture of happiness and misery. The face we see may be a double exposure, the forehead alternately puckering and smoothing out. There is a smile, but one that quivers. The eyes dance radiantly, but behind a film of moisture. It is a double exposure of trouble and pleasure.

At no other time in life does one want so much to have face and figure register favorably in the eyes of another person. Yet romantic love becomes quite cross-eyed at times! This is the natural consequence of close quarters. It is the attempt to focus at point-blank range. In films, a close-up shot can suggest the ardent gaze of a lover, even without showing us the hovering partner, provided the eyes are crossed for near focus. When this minimum interval is closed by embrace, the eyes are usually closed. In true love's embrace, love is truly blind!

Kittens and Wolves

A coquette is, by definition, a woman who endeavors to attract the amorous attention of men. It is interesting to note that the word stems from a very common French word—*coq*—and the allusion of coquetry is to the

proverbial strutting of the cock, a strictly male performance. It would appear that either male or female may behave coquettishly. The important thing in coquetry is that the effort to attract amorous attention must be without affection. Alexander Pope phrased it like this:

> As some coy nymph her lover's warm address
> Not quite indulges nor can quite repress.

Typical of the coquette is a lighthearted smile of playfulness and the modest shrinking from approach or familiarity.

Flirting is more bold, and either male or female may play the flirt. It has the jaunty touch. It deals playfully with love. The flirt is playing lover for sport. But if enticement is practiced without sportiveness and from lustful passion only, we see a rather different expression on the face. Most often, it is the one resentfully referred to as a leer. This is a sly glance. The face may wear a calculating or even fiendish grin of pleasure, or it may be set in grim earnestness. Singleness of purpose is indicated by steady gaze—eyes that remain fixed on the object of lust—and by partly lowered lids that help to confine the vision to the one and only object. But the lecherous leer is a way of glancing sidelong or obliquely, seeming to avoid eye contact. This may seem sneaky; it may seem candid— depending on one's point of view. (Without realizing it, you will probably leer at a person for whom you feel contempt.) The lustful leer is not so much avoiding eye contact as announcing that the interest is carnal rather than social. The leer is most effective when the brows are raised high, accentuating the full downward sweep of upper eyelids. Vision is actually blurred by the eyelashes. But the eyes remain fixed on the object of lust, and so they push forcibly upward against the drawn upper lids. If you are trying right now to leer, you must feel this pressure—the bulging cornea of the eye pushing up against the downward drive of the upper eyelid. And don't forget to raise your brows. The sultry leer is, commonly enough, a momentary resort of the flirt. After all, the flirt is on the lookout for an attractive partner in amorous diversions, not an adversary for a game of chess!

Established Love

The face of established love is not distinctive. We perceive love in many ways. It is there in the moments of beaming adoration, of sober reflection, of grave anxiety, and of rollicking fun. But we perceive love only as behavior in the relationship of two people. It is their mutual bond of intimacy and concern. So we arrive here at something of a paradox. Adult love—the most universally treasured of all experiences—is faceless. Adult love is steady and secure, and therefore tranquil.

> The night has a thousand eyes,
>   And the day but one;
> Yet the light of the bright world dies
>   With the dying sun.
>
> The mind has a thousand eyes,
>   And the heart but one;
> Yet the light of a whole life dies
>   When love is done.

Francis William Bourdillon

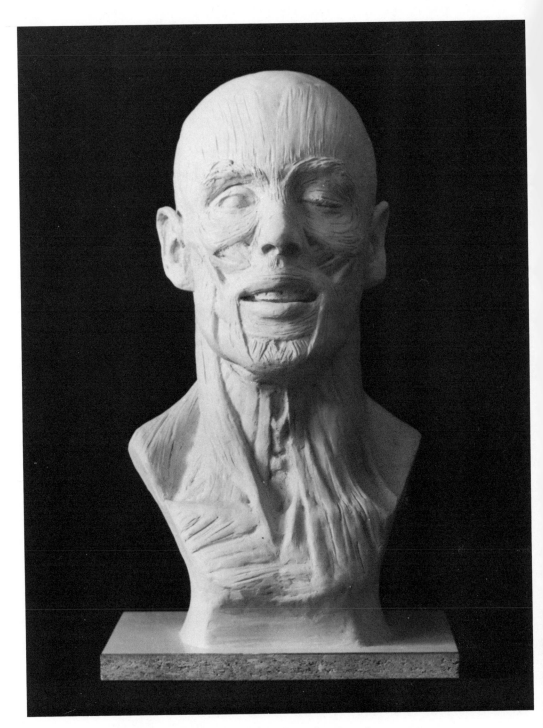

Plate III Sculptured Muscles of Head and Neck, Front View.

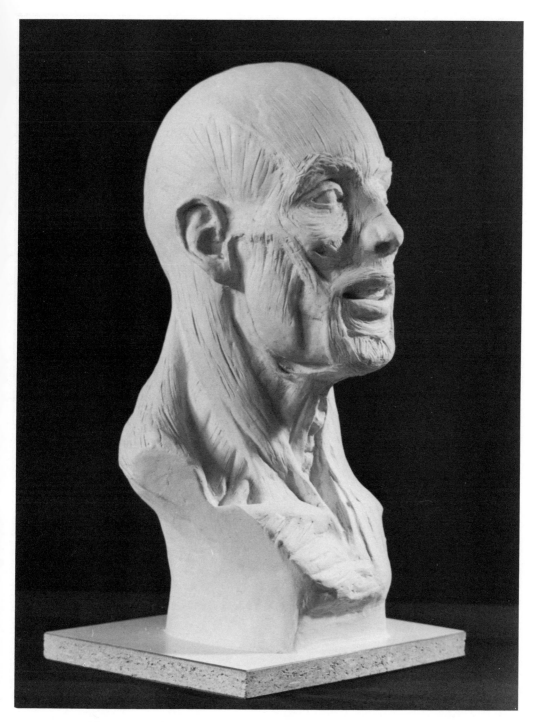

Plate IV Sculptured Muscles of Head and Neck, from Right Side.

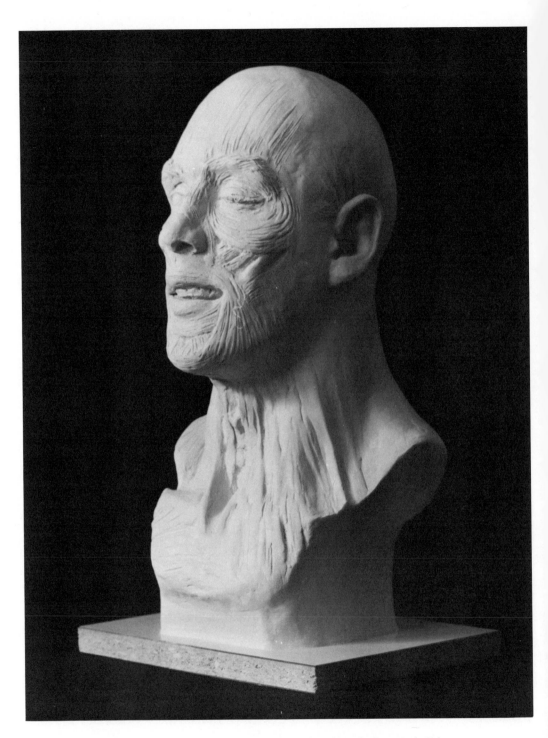

Plate V   Sculptured Muscles of Head and Neck, from Left Side.

Plate VI Infant Screaming. Plates VII and VIII show two more views. The event of being born is coupled right away with insistent demands for attention. Many features of facial expression are derived from the infant's preparation for a scream. The signal of *distress* is inescapable. See Chapter Three for details.

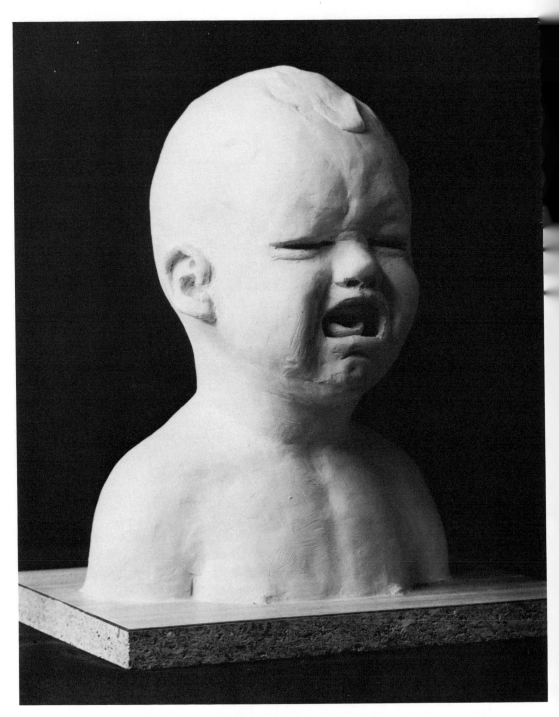

Plate VII Infant Screaming.

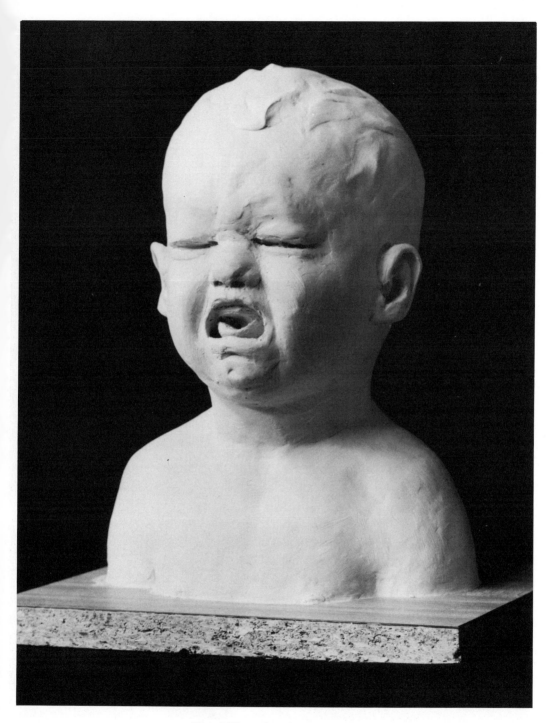

Plate VIII Infant Screaming.

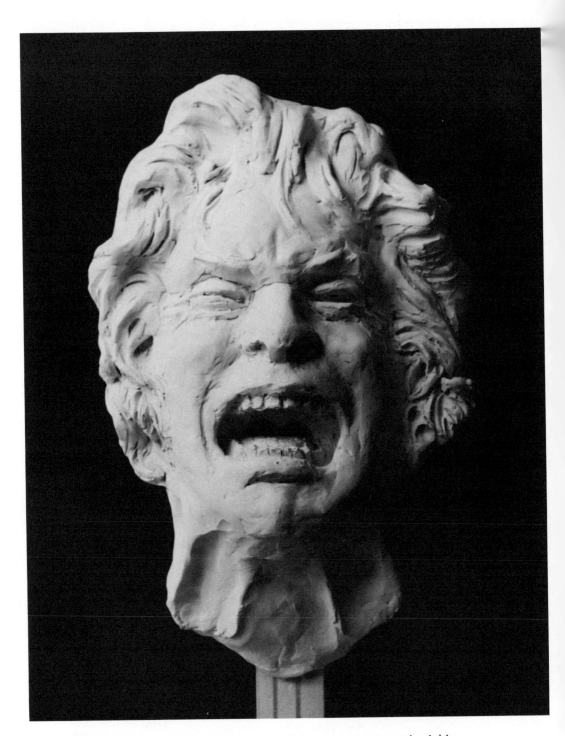

Plate IX Screaming Adult. Perhaps a rabble-rouser, a noisy and voluble merry-maker, or just a stubborn bigot. This is the petulant, squalling brat grown to adulthood. What is seen here is the countenance of grievous anger and rage, or possibly one of frantic alarm, yet possibly too the countenance of frivolity and explosive mirth. Learn about *violent expiration* in Chapter Three.

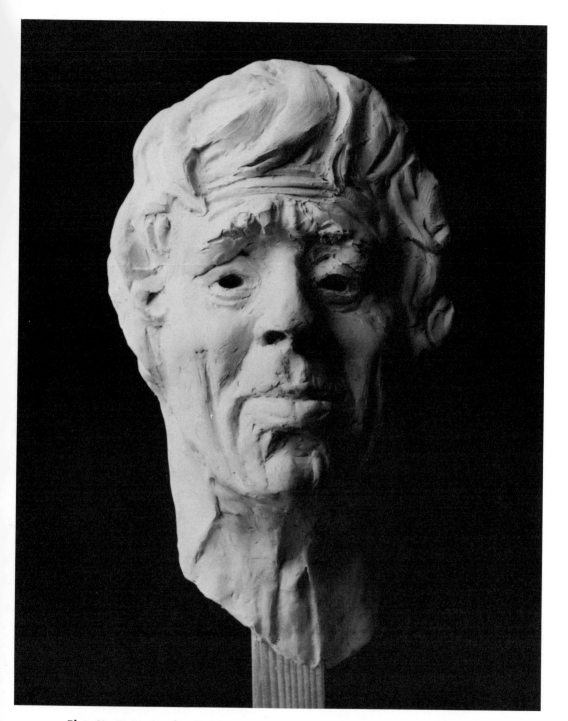

Plate X   Dejection / Melancholy. Traces of the aftermath of screaming can be seen in this doleful and disconsolate face. There is a crestfallen sadness here, the compromise with mute and noble dreams. It lies in the downward extension of the lower face, tempered by the upward rise of the brow. Think of a tug of war between forehead above and jaw below pulling in opposite directions.

Plate XI High Spirits / Merriment. The mood here is elevated to unadulter-
ated *pleasure*. Imaginary hooks seem to pull the corners of the mouth backward toward the rear of the head. At the same time, the mouth may be
upturned and lips rise higher against the teeth. Discover the significance of
a smooth forehead!

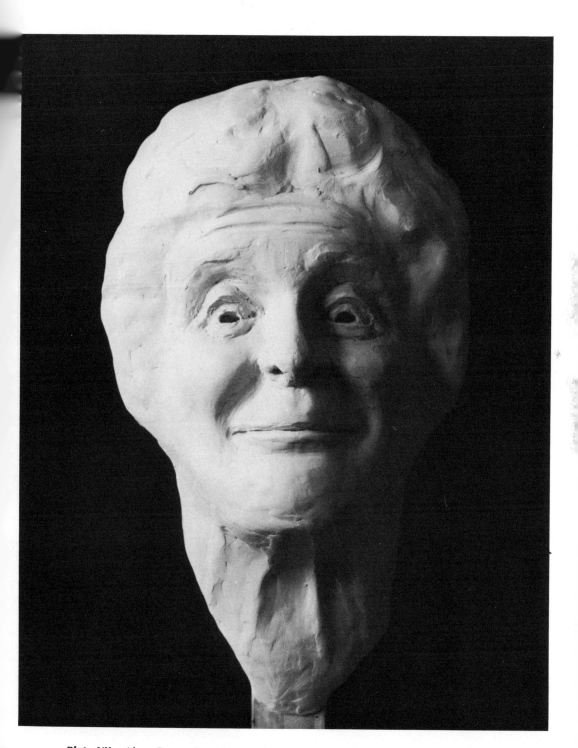

Plate XII Alert Constraint. The notable feature here is firm resolve and constraint, dominating a face of pleased attention. It may be that she must withhold for the moment some piece of good news or an exciting secret. Her cooperative determination is there in lips that would seem to be welded together. Try sealing your own lips on a perfectly horizontal line. No other feature can be so extended from left to right.

Plate XIII Facial Armor. At first glance a demure young woman. On closer study it might be arrogant disdain. The face is, in effect, locked up against the rude intrusion of life's vulgarities. Lips are pursed; eyelids are lowered almost totally; even nostrils are constricted. It is a shutting out of realities. And so it is a stage set for dreaming—the libidinous dreams of youth and the nostalgic dreams of old age. Try to do all this with a smooth forehead.

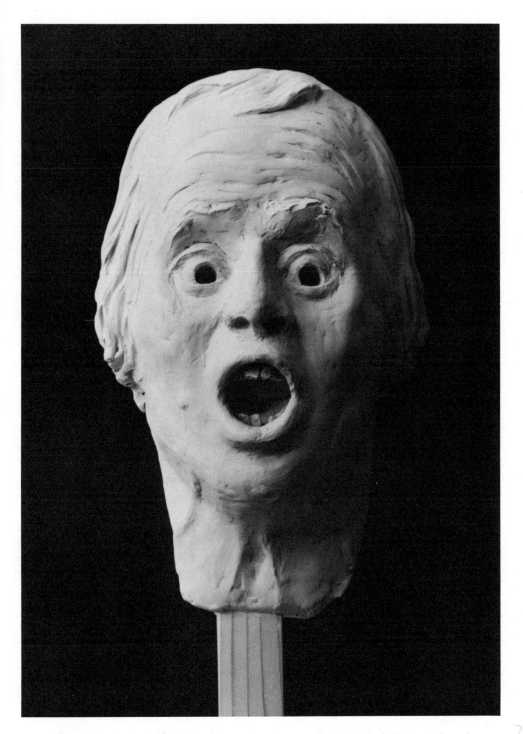

Plate XIV Surprise / Alarm. The wide-open mouth of *disbelief* is combined with the wide-open staring eyes of *astonishment*, eyes that search for an explanation. What would it take to change this to a simple gaping yawn?

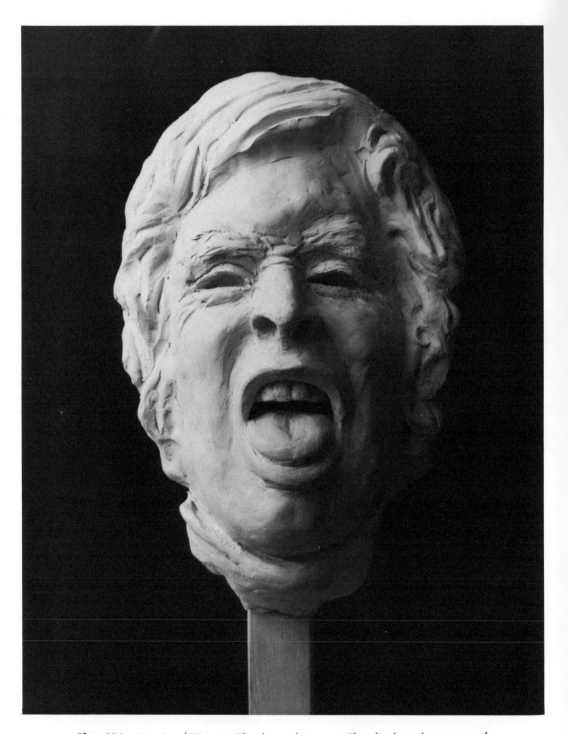

Plate XV Aversion / Disgust. The face of nausea. The display of upper teeth tells us the stage is set for throwing up. Both unfit food and unfit people can arouse *aversion*. Unacceptable social encounters may result in haughty *indignation*. *Loathing* and *hatred* are its extreme forms. Mere *distaste* and *repugnance* are its blander forms. Can you think of a useful reason for sticking out the tongue?

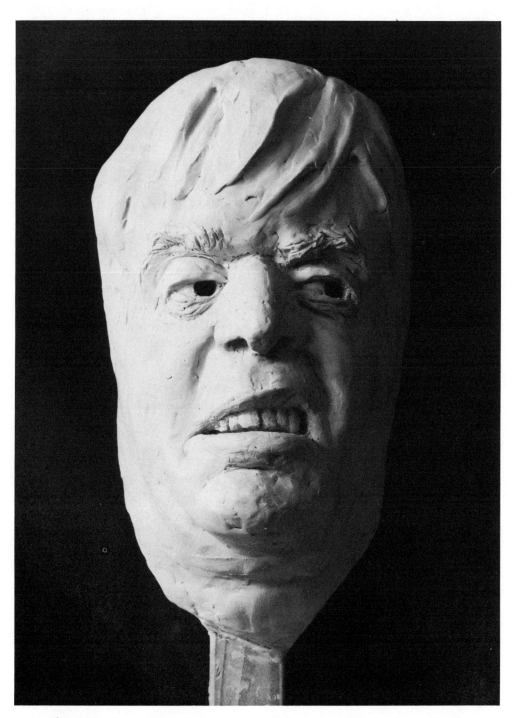

Plate XVI Anger / Rage. Intense *anger* will fix the eye relentlessly on the adversary, and the curling of the upper lip allows for exhibition of the canine tooth (eye tooth), once specially adapted for tearing into flesh. This snarl, as with the fixation of the eye, usually occurs on the side facing one's opponent. Try it.

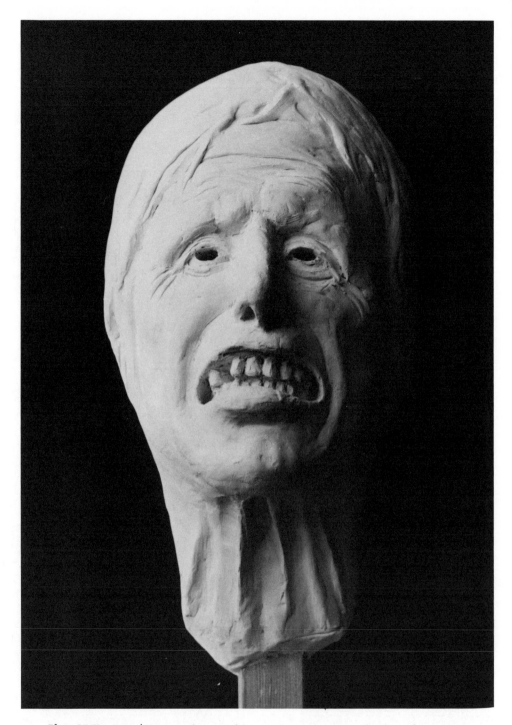

Plate XVII Fear / Terror. This pitiable creature of misery displays the scant-
ness of a minimal life. Here is one whose lot has been little more than to
subsist and endure. A revealing feature is the upper face of exhaustion with
weary, half-lowered eyelids. The downturned mouth betrays the need to cry
out in *agony*. (For suffering to the point of exhaustion, see Chapter Five.) Has
it occurred to you that suffering may wear a grin? (See Chapter Twelve.)

Plate XVIII Pain / Exhaustion. Just listen for a moment. Maybe you will hear the spasmodic groans of *pain* coming from one weakened by torture and fatigue. This man stares out aimlessly into space. Observe the eyes about to disappear under lids, revealing some white of eyeball below each disc of iris. Cover his forehead wrinkles, eyebrows, and upper lids—and see how very much the face has changed into what could be the dedicated choir leader! How are you at making a square mouth?

CHAPTER EIGHT

DOING A
DOUBLE TAKE

Egad!

As children, most of us came to think of a surprise as a sudden, unexpected delight—a package tied with ribbon, a newborn puppy, or the family's plans for a day at the circus. Sudden disappointments were unexpected too. But, for some reason, a surprise was nearly always a pleasure. The very word itself seemed loaded with a magic overtone that made the sulkiest child take notice. Even as adults, most of us continue to associate surprise mostly with merriment. "What a pleasant surprise!" you say; only rarely, "What an awful surprise!" The unhappy turn of events you are most apt to call a disappointment or a letdown.

You are surprised when you are taken unaware. The incident or idea must be sudden and unexpected, or contrary to what you had expected. And that is all. Probably you would be surprised, as you read along here, to stumble upon 十七世紀至十九世紀中葉中國帆船在東南亞洲航運和商業上．Unless you had scanned this page in advance, you were unprepared for a string of Chinese characters. But so gentle was the surprise that you only paused in your track and read on. Many of your daily surprises are no more breathtaking than this.

What takes you unaware could be anything from a typographical error to a pair of icy hands circling your neck. Or a gunshot at close range. When a loud gunshot is unexpected, the body assumes for an instant what psychologists call the startle pattern. This is a reflex pattern that creates what seems to be a defensive posture. In the face, it is observed (by high-speed camera) that the eyes blink and the mouth is drawn partway into a grin. You will be able to explain both blink and grin on the basis of your reading in Chapter Three. But let us not tangle here with the highly technical subject of flash reflexes. We'll have to dispense with the popguns and explosions. Nor can we include in this chapter the kind of surprise that may be mixed with fear and terror.

Incidental Intelligence

Inconsequential surprise is likely to raise the upper eyelids and no more. You may respond with raised lids to unusual information, especially that which seems to go against common knowledge or common sense—the truth-is-stranger-than-fiction type of surprise. But the information must not be important to you. Here are some examples. Try to note what your face is doing at the reading of the last line or two in each example.

> Unless you remember your chemistry, you might raise your lids on hearing that there are two metals lighter than water. And they melt *below* the boiling point of water!
> (Sodium and potassium.)

> Unless you remember your genetics, you may find it somewhat surprising that the blue-eyed man and his blue-eyed wife whom you see walking with the brown-eyed child may be the child's uncle and aunt but rarely his or her father and mother!
> (Blue eyes are a recessive trait.)

> Occasionally, an unborn child may cry out while still within the uterus!
> (The cause: rupture of membrane admitting air into the uterus.)

Are your eyes growing bigger? Read on.

> Human infants are sometimes born with tails! This is a matter of medical record and can be verified by photographs. The presence of a tail at birth is not unreasonable when one considers that all human embryos have tails—relatively as long and as thick as an alligator's tail, disappearing a few months before birth—ordinarily, that is. By the time an embryo is an inch long, its tail has been consigned to oblivion Yet the freakish thing happens now and then—little Elmer arrives complete with tail and the muscles to wag it!

Bewitched, Bothered, and Bewildered

The most illuminating study of surprise is in the realm of the unexpected which seems unaccountable—the *inexplicable surprise*. Here you find it

difficult—momentarily, at least—to comprehend what has just occurred. You are baffled, like old Rip Van Winkle. A good example of the inexplicable surprise would be to go shopping on what you assumed was a regular business day only to find the stores closed up tight. Or let's say your purse or wallet disappeared from the table where you left it, but the money it contained was still there. *Bewilderment* is a confusion of the mind owing to one's inability to comprehend. Contriving such confusion is the very art of the conjurer and the ventriloquist. They set out deliberately to deceive you. And when it's of no consequence whatsoever, this kind of deception may prove entertaining.

Earlier in this chapter, we noted that surprises can be either pleasant or unpleasant. There is, of course, a neutral ground where surprises seem to have neither happy nor unhappy flavors. Indeed, only in this neutral frame of reference can we isolate the facial pattern of surprise. Back there when you went shopping and found the stores closed, the trouble pattern formed above your big, incredulous eyes. If you followed the conjurer's clean, deft movements of legerdemain, or if you observed the rapidity of conversational exchange between ventriloquist and dummy, the grin of delight stretched out beneath those same wide eyes. It is not easy to confine surprise to the neutral ground. Surprise itself is fleeting and will turn promptly to pleasure, puzzlement, or dismay. But, so far, the common denominator seems to be those wide ping-pong eyes.

Brows Do More Than Collect Dust

If you were asked why you keep your eyes open, the obvious answer would be "to see." If you were then asked why, at times, you widen your eyes into a stare, you would reply that it would be "to see *better.*" Let's check that right here. Look up from this book at something straight ahead. Concentrate on keeping all your facial muscles relaxed. Imagine that your face is utterly paralyzed. Or think of your head as just an empty balloon. Without moving your eyes, take note of how much you see, even fuzzily, above the point where you are looking. Imagine now that every part of your face is still paralyzed except the upper eyelids. The only possible movement is to raise the eyelids just a fraction. As you do so, keep a smooth forehead. By alternate raising and lowering of upper eyelids, you can compare the original with the increased field of vision. (You raise the upper lid as if it were a theater curtain by contracting a small muscle descending to the eyelid rim from a position close above the eyeball on the ceiling of the bony eye socket.)

Now, as before, fixing your gaze straight ahead, once more raise the upper lids high and keep them raised for a few seconds. It's a muscular strain, isn't it? Can you feel the fatigue setting into those little lid muscles? Now, with lids still up there, raise your eyebrows. Do you feel the reinforcement? Your forehead muscle has contracted to wrinkle up the forehead skin into four or five horizontal lines like a music staff without the notes. The brow skin was pulled up high, and this, naturally, pulled on the skin of the upper eyelids. Not only does brow raising facilitate lid raising, but it also further increases the field of vision. Eyebrow hairs are like protective hedgerows planted to shield the eyes from above—from falling dust, the rain, and brilliant sunshine. But in performing this service they must also interfere with the view of things above. Thus, brow raising enlarges the visual field momentarily to its maximum diameter.

The next time you have occasion to be on the street in the wee hours of the morning, look for the fellow who is fighting off drowsiness until he can make it home. You don't doubt his drowsiness because the eyelids look heavy and low. But where, you ask, is the evidence of any effort to resist drowsiness? It's right there on his forehead. Since the eyelids are fatigued and relaxed, the forehead muscle has come to the rescue. Until the sleepy fellow can reach his bedside, this forehead muscle will substitute for lid muscles. It is a case not of enlarging the visual field but of maintaining an adequate field. Accordingly, in the presence of your guests, it is scarcely less rude to sustain a wrinkled forehead than to indulge in a yawn. Luckily, the authorities on etiquette have overlooked this particular.

Veni, Vidi, Vici

There seems to be the most intimate connection between vision and comprehension, or between what we see with our eyes and what we grasp with our minds. One homespun phrase puts it this way: "Seeing is believing." And how commonly we catch ourselves asking "Do you see?" or answering "I see." Not for a second are we referring to eyesight, but rather to understanding. We are speaking figuratively, but the inference is there, that having seen it makes it so. How natural and how obvious that we should widen our eyes if a strangely shaped animal comes into our field of vision. The momentary inability to visualize or comprehend an idea also causes us to widen our eyes for a more complete and unobstructed view. In the great mass of our experience we have learned the most about things by getting up close for a detailed examination, or by looking around us for other clues. Through habit and long association we

are compelled to enlarge our visual field, even though the immediate problem is not strictly an optical one.

The patient brows stand ready at all times to help by drawing upward out of the way. So sensitively are they triggered that they do not discriminate between visual and nonvisual surprises. They are like mousetraps that care not a whit if the disturbance of bait is a mouse or a golf ball. So up the brows go, on the chance that some welcome clue will be revealed.

Ask a young child to imagine how it must feel to walk across clouds in the sky. Then watch the child's eyes open wide and the brows rise on the forehead. This pattern is almost inevitable as he conjures up pictures in his mind. It's a sign hanging on his head that says "Woolgathering—Do Not Disturb." The brow element, in particular, is a familiar accompaniment to quiet reverie or daydreaming.

But what about arching just one eyebrow? This is a feat that few people can perform well. The forehead muscle that pulls up the eyebrows is really divided a bit at the center, something like a part in your hair. Each eyebrow has a separate half of the muscle fibers. The ability to exercise one half independently of the other is mostly an accidental development. Many of your body movements are more successfully executed by one side than by the other. For instance, don't you find that you favor a certain side of your face for winking? Probably the same side is favored for snarling. Arms and legs are notoriously asymmetrical in bony and muscular refinements. You may have noticed this in the fit of a pair of shoes or gloves. Or consider which hand you use for writing, or for buttoning and unbuttoning your clothing. Such asymmetry should not be surprising, then, at the forehead. The favored brow will usually rise a little higher than its mate. A small band of muscle fiber at the root of the nose runs upward to fasten to the inner end of each eyebrow. If this tightens on the upraised brow, it will restrain it and accent the upward lift of the opposite brow. In this case, there is only half a "washboard" of forehead wrinkles—over the arched eyebrow, of course.

The raising of only one eyebrow qualifies the aspect of surprise. The expression becomes one of feigned surprise. Because of the restraint involved, we must look upon this as indicating reservation. What we call a skeptical look will rely chiefly on this device of the single arched brow.

Raised brows can be a part of many different attitudes, but the reason is almost always the same: to increase the visual field. In Chapter Four we saw that forehead contraction to raise brows was necessary to undo the screaming pattern. And since that pattern involved squeezed-shut eyes, undoing meant opening the eyes, so the reason still holds. In the

same chapter, we found raised brows in the effort to recall. Again, the reason is the same. The only exception was in Chapter Two. There we discovered the brows rising as an act of empathy. Where vigorous effort was directed toward achieving height or reaching to high places—as in star-gazing at the heavens—the brows perform a thoroughly real assistance by rising up out of the way. In spite of all this, the fact remains that raised eyebrows have always been and will continue to be synonymous with surprise itself.

What you see below may suggest a variety of ways to say "O"—possibly, too, a variety of circumstances in which it might be sounded. Some of them might be uphill sounds and others downhill. Such exclamations could be associated with addressing a person or with expressing pain, joy, grief, surprise, relief, fear, or desire. It could be crying out in protest, in reproach, in complaint. "O" has many sounds indeed, not the least of which is "Oh—oh!"

The Ring of Lips

The sound of "O" can be given either of two glissando (sliding) inflections: "OH" like this: 🎵 Or "OH" like this: 🎵 The up scale is like an airplane that takes off and never lands. It is left dangling; it invites further comment. The down scale seems to be a reply, a final statement putting us back to rest. Together, in quick succession, the two scales would look like this: 🎵 Or a sound diagrammed thus: ⌒ When uttered as speech, we hear an overtone of concern: "Oh? Oh" as when a speeding driver might spot, in his rear-view mirror, a police patrol car in pursuit with flashing lights.

At this point of the discussion, you may feel you have grown callused to surprise. So it may not ruffle you now to hear that the exclamation "Oh" seems to hail directly from the need for full lungs of air in sudden alarm. You can appreciate that a person having cause for alarm would need oxygen instantly. Any alarm is a signal to go into action without delay. Just think of your bedside clock. Probably the first reaction of the sleeper to the buzz of the alarm clock is to suck in a volume of air. The very act of reaching out or hopping from the bed to shut off the hellish clatter will demand a drastic and instantaneous step-up in body processes. Increasing the oxygen supply to the blood is one of nature's devices for meeting the emergency. It is the gasp—the drawing of air forcibly down into the lungs. In Chapter Five, this was seen as a reiterated convulsion, called sobbing. A single spasm is just a gasp. Probably, it's just the first sudden plunge into deep breathing.

However accurate are these physiological details, two related events appear to have reasonable explanations: the inhalation or gasp of surprise taken through an O-shaped mouth, and the exhalation which follows with the accompaniment of an audible "O." The utterance may be varied somewhat: "Ho!" "Huh!" "Hah!" "Ah!" Even "A-Hah" and "O-Ho!"

Perhaps it is not too far-fetched to think of a smoker blowing smoke rings. He draws in a quantity of smoke. Then, with his tongue centered behind the circle of lips, he nudges intermittent puffs of smoke outward. In uttering surprise, our tongues are also centered far behind a circle of lips. The only difference is that we drive the air outward by a blast from the lungs rather than by gentle tongue protrusion. So it can readily be seen that surprise, through long association, might impel us to gasp for air with a circular mouth, as well as to raise eyelids and brows. With such a face, we have made every effort to achieve maximum visibility and immediate supply of oxygen for action if necessary.

There is a photograph of an old man who (so it is reported) has just "awakened" from hypnosis. Many years before, he had lost the power of speech through shellshock in World War I. While hypnosis was being induced, the man was instructed to start counting slowly. During the hypnotic state he was assured that the power of speech was returning. And, according to the report, this man did awaken to hear himself counting aloud! The close-up photograph made at his awakening is a classic example of joyous bewilderment. In addition to the high, slanting brows and greatly uplifted eyelids, the mouth is gaping wide and drawn sharply into a grin. In this special instance, how wrong—technically—to say he has been struck dumb, although his surprise could have been nothing short of dumbfounding!

Shock

Except for the unique example just given, speechlessness goes hand in hand with surprise of great magnitude: *amazement* and *stupefaction*. It may seize either the survivor of a brush with death or the heir to a colossal fortune. A gaping mouth or just parted lips that have nothing to say can be the sign of shock. Upper eyelids will, for a time, be high to expose the full disc of the colored ring (iris) of the eye. But they must soon lower from fatigue, whereas the state of shock (sometimes with parted lips) can persist for hours.

Emotional shock bears a strong resemblance to any other type of shock—that which stems from injury, poisoning, hemorrhage, and so on. A general diminishing of most body processes sets in; circulation may be lowered, perhaps even critically; a cold pallor comes into the face and extremities; the pupils of the eyes dilate; the mind grows sluggish. The important exception, according to my own observations, is that the profuse sweating of ordinary physical shock is not a usual symptom in emotional shock.

Finally, there is a type of shock that transforms the face into a frozen mask with a lifeless gaze. I was told about an incident that took place at an overseas military post during World War II. A young lieutenant, recently married, had received a recorded message made by his bride back home. He took the recording to a place on the post that was equipped with a phonograph. About to go on duty, he left it there unplayed, intending to hear it later. The chap who tells this story stopped by shortly after the lieutenant's departure. Inadvertently, he picked up the lieutenant's recording, unaware of its personal nature and wanting only to hear a little music. He started it playing on the phonograph. This turned out to be sacrilege enough. But to make matters far worse, his instant discovery was that the phonograph was wired into a public address system, used at certain hours of the day to carry popular music to the entire post. So out it blared over the great amplifier system: the bride's soft and tender words of endearment, the most touching and intimate vows of her love. So utterly stupefied was this chap that he froze on the spot, unable even to take off the recording until it had played to a finish. Be assured, this fellow was neither coarse nor insensitive. Yet, asked to describe his feelings, he said he couldn't remember feeling anything whatsoever. Knowing what we know now about shock, this lack of feeling should not "surprise" us.

CHAPTER NINE

CODFISH AND CHOCOLATE SAUCE

The Recipe

Cut into half-inch cubes
a large codfish
Dredge the cubes well with
baking soda
Sauté for 20 minutes in
mineral oil
Remove from fire and combine with
1 pint raspberry juice
½ cup mustard
1 cup maple syrup
Drench with
melted chocolate
Garnish with
chopped pickles

Now that you've had fair warning, let's get down to business. It will be the disagreeable business of exploring the disagreeable. Only by exploring it can you truly understand a number of very common facial patterns. Back in Chapter Five, you found several ways to induce tears. Some of them were not exactly gentle. One of these techniques was throat tickling. It is guaranteed to do more than produce tears—it induces retching. As a matter of fact, it is retching that brings on the tears. In Chapter Three, you investigated the subject of violent expiration. Most of the varieties were discussed: choking, screaming, sneezing, and so on. But retching was discreetly omitted from the list. Some people have delicate stomachs and are highly suggestible in gastronomic matters. Yet retching is a charter member of the Violent Expiration Club. There is no better representative to be found.

The Nauseous Feeling

You must have experienced it at one time or another—the uneasy predicament of being nauseated. Many people localize the queazy sensation at the pit of the stomach, which is just below the breastbone. A hand clasped there over the stomach is sometimes a deliberate gesture for showing disgust. Generally, people describe the unpleasant sensation as a sinking feeling in that region of the body. There is good reason to call it sinking, because the stomach has actually been observed to drop as much as a couple of inches with the onset of nausea. It is also very common to localize the sensation of nausea at the back of the throat, the pharynx. Such nausea might be described as a feeling that the lower throat is being distended or widened as if crammed with food. Evidently, the stomach and esophagus walls are being subjected to a stretch (mostly downward) that exerts a tension on their nerve fibers. This might explain the continuity of sensation from stomach up to throat. Outwardly, one feels uneasy and may salivate profusely, even perspire. Sometimes, there is a forced effort to swallow, as if to reverse the impending upward heave. Very likely, the upper lip will be drawn upward. But the slightest trace of upper lip retraction announces *distaste*. Look into your mirror and notice, when you retract your own upper lip, how widely the nostrils open, and how marked are the furrows that swing from the wings of the nose down to the corners of the mouth.

Retching

The mechanics of retching provide a means of ejecting stomach contents from the body, either when the contents are unfit for digestion or when the stomach itself is not in condition to function properly.

To empty a plastic bottle, it is not always necessary to invert it. Pressure on the sides of the bottle will force its contents up and out through the opening at the top. The stomach may be emptied in a similar way. Compression must be exerted from all directions except that of the opening for escape upward. Retching is primarily the convulsive and violent contraction of the stomach walls, aided greatly by a sudden and equally violent descent (contraction) of the diaphragm and tightening of abdominal muscles. The exit from stomach into intestine is closed most forcibly, but the entrance above remains relaxed, as well as the entire esophagus. A few such spasms can empty the stomach most effectively.

The entrance to the windpipe is momentarily closed, so this inhibits respiration. Also closed is the entrance to the nasal cavity at the back of

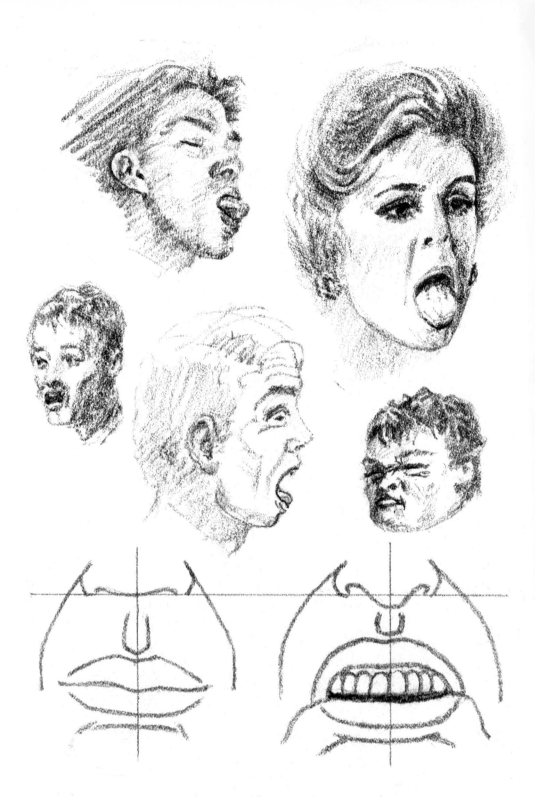

RETRACTION OF UPPER LIP

the throat. Consequently, there is but a single highway left open for escape of the offensive matter—that of the open mouth. It is interesting that the larynx (Adam's apple), which is the front wall of the throat, is momentarily drawn forward. Obviously, this serves to further dilate the passageway behind. Probably it accounts for the sensation of lower throat distention mentioned earlier. Every possible assistance is given to insure an effective evacuation.

So far, we have taken the open mouth detail for granted. It should be clear enough that the upper lip rises toward the nose in order to get out of the way. The lower lip is thrust forward as the tongue rides out over it. Presumably, an extended tongue helps to channel the vomitus (as medical texts politely refer to it) and expedite its delivery to the outside. And certainly it reduces the possibility of a very messy mouth.

Protrusion of the tongue is apparently an instinctive movement to dump out from the mouth anything that seems unfit to swallow. Quite naturally, it would form a part of the reflex pattern in retching. Little children who stick out their tongues at each other in great contempt are saying, in effect, "I can't stomach you. You're so nasty it makes me feel like vomiting!"

Naturally, you are waiting eagerly for a chance to practice retching! Just draw a very deep breath. At the top of your inhalation, close the air passage in your throat completely, but leave your lips and teeth loosely separated. The tip of the tongue should lie out on the lower lip, and the upper lip should rise toward the nose. Now squeeze downward with your chest wall, as if trying to push your lungs and heart down into your abdomen. Even forcing your shoulders downward will help. All this is done to bring great pressure upon your stomach and thus to compel it to give up its contents. If you practice a few times, you will readily be able to summon up that certain feeling. The expiration, of course, would be delayed until vomiting is induced.

The act of retching has already been referred to as a charter member in the Violent Expiration Club. This is to say that retching will be a notorious producer of tears. You don't have to be nauseated to prove this. Just tickle around the back of your tongue and throat with a cotton swab. But be prepared for dry heaving and a flood of tears!

It is curious that the facial patterns derived from retching do not seem to involve watering of the eyes, as may be the case with patterns of grief and hilarity that derive from similar explosive forces. Mere nausea, with all its sweat and uneasiness, lacks the accompaniment of moist eyes. Possibly this can be explained by the fact that we don't retch frequently enough to habituate the tears with the disagreeable feeling. We do, however, cling to the squeezed-shut eyes that go with any violent expiration. And so the expressions of extreme distaste are bound to show wrinkling of the nose and the flesh around the eyes.

On the Offensive

Experiment has shown that the tone of stomach muscles increases in response to a disgusting stimulus. This fact alone places disgust apart from all other forms of unpleasantness (which are known to decrease the muscle tone of the stomach). To have your face suddenly splattered with ice water or confetti would cause you only to look startled or annoyed. To knowingly have your face splattered with a dead jellyfish would most certainly produce some trace of the facial pattern for retching. Obviously, then, we are dealing in this chapter with a form of unpleasantness that has its own special trademark. It will be enlightening if we inquire about what exactly constitutes a stimulus of retching.

The stomach is an extremely sensitive organ. It must be sensitive because it has a grave responsibility. It is the gateway to the bloodstream, where every morsel of food must be certified as fit and proper for digestion. Harmful substances must be identified and hastily neutralized or rejected.

Early in your life you caught on to a fundamental fact of good health: your food must be unspoiled and free from contamination. You learned about decomposition, poisons, and disease-producing bacteria. In most cases, it was not necessary to taste a sample of food to detect spoilage. Your eyes and your nose could warn you in advance. Moldy bread very plainly showed evidence of plant life. Tainted meat had a putrid odor. Sour milk had a curdled look and a rancid odor. Rotten fruit not only smelled fermented but was visibly past its prime. As for insects, worms, or other dubious passengers in the morsel of food, your eyes came to be always on the alert. Automatically, you inspected every spoonful before it became a mouthful. For this reason, you are still reluctant to swallow unseen food in the dark. It has been asked what is worse than to see a fly in your sandwich. And the answer is to see half a fly! This is no joke. It is not surprising that the sight or smell of spoiled or contaminated food should readily evoke the facial preparation for retching—the raised upper lip and widened nostrils, the wrinkled nose and squinted eyes, and the protruded lower lip and tongue.

Prehistoric humans certainly knew nothing about the facts of decay, fermentation, and poisons. Probably, without this knowledge, they had a more practiced ability to regurgitate food that caused distress. When

THESE TEETH
MAY SHOW

LOWER TEETH
COVERED

one considers how easily an animal can throw up its meal, it is not difficult to imagine that those prehistoric people could do likewise. But you live in the age of fast freight, deep freeze, irradiation, vacuum sealing, and proprionates (additives to retard spoilage). You are spared a multitude of unpleasant discoveries. There is an abundance of packaged food available with guarantees—those familiar commercial claims of "sealed-in goodness."

Garbage is food but is regarded as already spoiled or contaminated, or as containing unpalatable trimmings. On this account, you will see some people raise the upper lip slightly when scraping off dishes after a meal. The sight of regurgitated food or the smell of sour vomit, even the sound of someone retching, can be the most potent of lip raisers. The communal vomiting of passengers aboard an ocean liner on heavy seas is probably as much a chain reaction as it is a direct consequence of the ship's instability. Again, with the knowledge that the vomited matter is or was food, there is the unavoidable association of eating it.

Unusual foods can, in themselves, be triggers of retching. For many Americans, the popular raw fish dishes of Japan (sushi, sashimi, etc.) are regarded as unfit for consumption. In some countries of Central America, it is reported that a delicacy is roasted grasshoppers. And eating horse-flesh is not uncommon in European countries, although it raises a brow in the United States.

And Food Isn't All

If you are ahead of this discussion, you are calling to mind a host of things that arouse disgust yet are not in any sense items of food. It appears that any organic substance from within the body may arouse disgust: blood, spittle, mucus, phlegm, pus, excrement, sweat, and so on. You will surely find it difficult admitting to any association of such unsavory substances with the idea of swallowing them. But the fact remains that those substances were, at one time, taken into the body as food. Chemistry has wrought the transformation. Even the drinking of human milk would probably be a trifle offensive to anyone except the suckling infant.

It is curious that what is generally held as disagreeable by one group of people may not be at all repugnant to another group. This is eminently true in the culinary line. But consider the matter of body odor. We live in a fastidious society that frowns sternly on it. Cosmetic and pharmaceutical industries have helped to create the taboo by gentle suggestion and reminder. For Smellie Nellie, we are told, there can be no second date with Sweet Pete—all because she doesn't know about the magic of a certain deodorant. This must be quite different from the attitude prevailing in European courts during the Renaissance. Perfumes came into fashion again and again. But at various times they were banned or fell into disfavor. In any case, they were apparently employed by ladies and courtesans not as a measure to disguise body odor but rather for their own fragrances. Presumably, body odor was not necessarily offensive.

Another instance is the odor of the dried root of valerian. In the sixteenth century this was regarded as fragrant and was placed among clothes as a perfume. Today, ask your pharmacist to let you sniff the valerian on his shelf (either powdered root or fluid extract), and you will see for yourself what a thoroughly foul (and lingering) odor it has for modern nostrils. (However, it is conceivable that valerian may have actually become altered in the course of a few hundred years).

Decomposition or decay of any organism is apt to qualify as a stimulus of disgust. One thinks not only of maggots and slugs and a fetid stench, but also of general sliminess, ooze, and muck. It would be distasteful, but not far from accurate, to describe the decaying carcass of a rat as resembling—in texture—a portion of succulent meatloaf!

The Recoiling Hand

At this point, we should be well aware of the close connection between the reflex pattern of retching and the special senses of sight, taste, and smell. Yet there is a whole class of offensive things that can be experienced through the sense of touch, or the thought of being touched. This class of things is limited mostly to animal life that creeps, crawls, or slithers, and to a lesser extent some of the animals that swim or fly. Many people share in the abhorrence of snakes, snails, frogs, toads, lizards, spiders, innumerable insects, bats, and such weird creatures as the octopus.

What property do these varied animals have in common? It would seem to be what the mind conjures up as the prospective sensation of touching or being touched, notably the sensation of sliminess. Oddly, nothing could be much drier to the touch than a snake or a lizard. Sliminess, as we have seen, is the chief visible feature of animal decay. But, perhaps more than this, sliminess is foreign to our own dry skins and those of our domesticated animals. Add to this the element of liveliness—the squirming, wriggling, fluttering, or undulation, as the case may be—and the unpleasant sensation is doubled in intensity. People have a natural affinity and affection for many animals. So keenly is this felt by some that animal cages at the zoo must not only have bars to keep the animals in, but also rails to keep the people out!

Perhaps it has become instinctive in human nature to look upon all animals as potential pets and companions. If so, we could understand the conflict set up between viewing an octopus as something to be caressed affectionately and recoiling with a wry face at the mere thought of the slippery touch. There seems to be no clear evidence to suggest that little children are naturally revolted by the sight or touch of any particular animal. Fears and abhorrences result from unpleasant encounters such as stings, clutches, and bites, or from hearing about such encounters. Disgust would seem to be an exclusively human capacity, resulting from associations in the mind. Animals exhibit liking, disliking, or indifference, but not what we think of as disgust.

A corpse may incite disgust long before it decomposes. There is no stench, no ooze—just an inanimate sculpture that bears a frightful resemblance to the warm, living body. But a touch will tell you that the corpse is cool and waxy. You raise your lip in distaste and feel the urge to turn away. Why? Death may be sorrowful, but why should it be distasteful? Your sensibilities have been hurt, but why have they also been offended? Death can be as natural and as simple as birth. Birth, in fact, can be more messy than death. But any offense attending a healthy birth will be dispelled by the gladness and satisfaction of successful delivery. The corpse is quite another matter. And the sober face that gazes upon it can adopt the upper lip retraction without any disturbance to the turned-down mouth.

The distastefulness of death would seem to be explained by an element of something unnatural and unfamiliar to the sight or touch. You take breathing sounds and movements for granted and rarely notice them in the living. You take for granted the blinking and shifting of the eyes, ceaseless except in sleep. And you take for granted the warm springiness of flesh. When these life signs are no longer evident, the body assumes a stark strangeness. The atmosphere grows eerie, not unlike that of a wax museum. The dead body has given up its recent signs of life, whereas the wax figure in the museum—with all its skillful simulation of the shapes of life—has simply never acquired the vital signs.

To some people, any unusualness of an organic nature can be repulsive. Some find distasteful their first encounter with a praying mantis, an uncanny insect that looks like a twig and (unlike other insects) can turn its head around to follow a person's movements. Yet the mantis is a helpful little creature in controlling certain pest populations and is even purchased on the market for this purpose. Since the quality of mere peculiar-

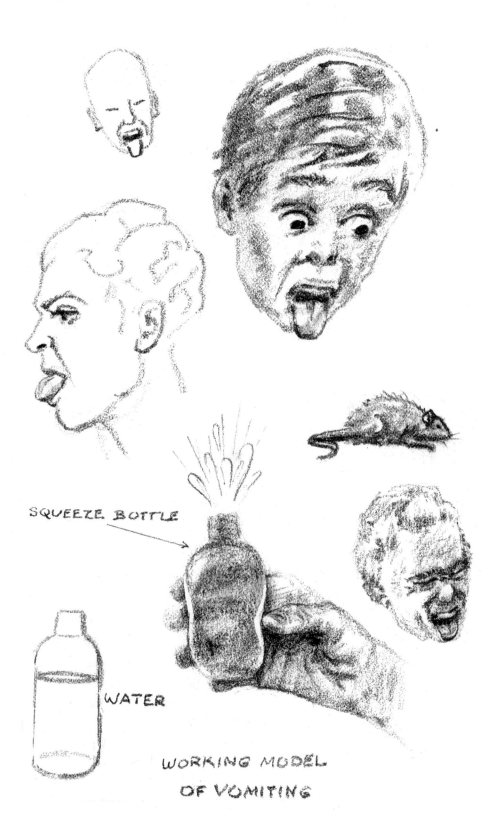

SQUEEZE BOTTLE

WATER

WORKING MODEL
OF VOMITING

ity in the taste or texture of your food is suspect for reasons of self-preservation, there is little difficulty in seeing how the upper-lip retraction might become habituated as a response to all organic strangeness. It is not required that the object arousing disgust must be actually seen, tasted, smelled, or touched. An image in the mind is sometimes sufficiently vivid to cause the response. So discussion of such unpleasant subjects is outlawed at the dinner table. If you have come this far in this chapter without an upset, you have already proved some resistance to revolting imagery.

Disgusting Behavior

Disgust, as a feeling expressed in the face, does not necessarily imply the offensiveness of spoilage or slime. In any realm of thought or experience where your sensibilities are offended, there is disgust. How many times have you been revolted by another person's behavior? The following traits of behavior might serve to refresh your memory: vanity, ostentation, arrogance, stinginess, greed, boorishness, curiosity, gaucherie, rudeness, vulgarity, snobbery, brutishness. Most of these traits are harmless but go against the grain of well-mannered people. Such traits provoke little more than aversion or scorn. But brutishness is another thing. It strikes between the eyes of any morally sensitive human being and arouses the fiercest kind of loathing. Drunkenness, too, can incite disgust, because it leads to foolishness, to the indignity of babbling talk and faltering conduct.

The foregoing inquiry into what things are nauseating and why should be enough to illuminate the expressions that stem from a retching face.

Dislike

Aversion is a dislike that is coupled with the desire to turn away from the offensive object. Its manifestation may be only the faintest tension in the upper lip. Consider how you might look if you were examining an open sore on a person's foot. *Loathing* is extreme aversion or abhorrence. You might be filled with loathing if the sore on the person's foot were crawling with maggots. When the object of aversion is regarded as mean or unworthy, there is *contempt.* Here, the raised upper lip is accompanied by arched brows and lowered eyelids. You might respond this way on having to submit to rude interrogation by some petty official. Your arched brows dramatize the idea that it's an effort even to look at this insignificant pest, and your lowered lids announce that he or she is unworthy of your attention. The brow and eyelid plan alone is contempt enough. But add to this a trace of upper-lip retraction and you have heaped insult upon injury, for the raised lip declares that you find this little worm of a person as repugnant as second-hand food.

Sneering

Derision is contemptuous laughter that makes sport of its victim. A sardonic smile is not a bona fide grin at all. The corners of the mouth may even turn down. But the cheeks push upward to pucker the lower eyelids, and they succeed in etching out the crow's-feet wrinkles. Actually, the corners of the mouth only appear to drop. It is the center of the mouth that rises, spreading out the nostrils and deepening the furrows beside them. So there it is, in disguise, the same old upper-lip retraction. Any illusion of genuine delight evaporates when we detect this nasty raising of the upper lip. The pattern is called a *sneer*. The smile becomes a mockery, its target a laughingstock.

The villain sneers fiendishly as he closes in on the helpless heroine to strangle her delicate throat. Do you want to play the role of the villain? Draw your upper lip against your nose and spread the nostrils wide, Add a broad grin, letting the upper front teeth show. Now you can start closing in. And you can approach with every assurance that she, too, will retract her upper lip!

Down a Turned-Up Nose

Toss your head way back, look down over your nose, and give a slight tug on your upper lip. Does that make you feel better? That is, better than other folks? *Arrogance* is this kind of overbearing affectation of superiority. It exalts unduly one's sense of self-importance. You might find this lofty pose among the would-be "blue bloods" who revere their ancestral trees, genealogies, and heraldry. You'll find it among ordinary "red bloods" who rate people by their titles, life styles, or properties. There is arrogance among the intellectuals, the aesthetes, those who have hobnobbed with celebrities, the dilettantes, the connoisseurs, the gourmets, the lovers of exclusiveness, the despisers of pedestrian ways.

Arrogance is only self-esteem pumped up with air. To gain a position of superiority—whether for brain, brawn, or prowess in drinking—is the aspiration of most of humanity. When a person gets carried away by a consciousness of superiority, he rejects those he would like to consider his inferiors. And we call his presumptuous behavior snobbery. His countenance takes the shape of arrogance. The puffed-up fellow is not content to keep his exalted station a secret. He cannot endure letting us go unaware of it. So his chin is held high to allow for a steep downward cast of eyes and an almost soporific droop of eyelids, punctuated by the arching brows. He says, in effect, "You are so far beneath me that I hardly see you." Quite plainly, stature is an important factor. The face of arrogance on a short man can be downright comical. Even with head thrust high, the short man's condescending downward glance may take in nothing higher than the other fellow's ankles. So he probably resorts to the sidelong glance. With this contemptuous leer, he looks beyond him into empty space. He suffers, perhaps, from lack of stature, yet he need not fail to make known his repugnance for others less exalted. The upward drag of his upper lip will suffice to indicate a foul taste—something like codfish and chocolate sauce.

CHAPTER TEN

FURNACE OF FURY

How to Hold Your Tongue

According to Rabelais, "He that has patience may compass anything." How is your patience? It's defined as your capacity for calm endurance under provocation. Let's challenge it right now.

Although the lines below appear to have words with jumbled letters, that is not exactly true. All the letters are in their correct order, but the letters of each word are separated by some letter not found in the word. For example, the word *example* might be shown as *ehxhahmhphlhe*. Can you read this hidden message?

Orwrirnrg tmo yeoeuer voiosouoaol awcwuwiwtwy aknkd
csesrsesbsrsasl ifnfgfefnfufiftfy, tuhuius mcecscscacgca
ixs njo lmomnmgmemr hbibdbdbebn.

If that was too easy, try this. The following lines can be read in the usual order from left to right, but not in the usual manner. You will have to spin the page to keep the train of thought. And some of the words are spelled backward. See what sense you can make of it.

Whatever pisdɾəsəs ᘓo o interferes ɥʇıʍ ʇɐɥʍ noʎ əɹɐ gniyrt ʇo do llıʍ

ʎouuɐ noʎ ɟı sʇı continuation o ɹədəʇıʇou səɹınbəɹ ɹnoʎ ecnaraebrof puɐ

deilpmi sı ɐu itself ʇıɯə ʇo əgɐssə oS lortnoc-fles o əsıɔɹəxə

pıuɯəusıou ɟo ecnayonna.

Were you determined to read the lines even though it was a nuisance to twirl the page around? What you found was not only an example of a nuisance but also a definition of one. Did you exhibit calm endurance under provocation? Or have you already ripped the page to shreds? By the way, what was your mouth doing?

To Be Hexed and Vexed

A nuisance is a kind of disturbance that is continuous or recurring at frequent intervals, such as a window rattling in the wind. You fight the impulse to speak out by sealing your lips in firm *Determination*. You say, in effect, "I will not let this thing get the best of me." We think of determination as a resolve to do something. Actually, the face of determination is a resolve only to remain silent. In Chapter Six, we mentioned the sealing of lips as part of the arch look. But there the feature was used lightheartedly to keep from giving away a secret. With determination, the lips are sealed to prevent the utterance of an oath or an angry remark. It seems doubtful that our early ancestors indulged in lip sealing for this purpose. The caveman may not have bothered to glare at his mate with lips sealed in restraint when she offered him rabbit instead of mammoth. He must have grunted aloud his displeasure and flung the rabbit to the wolves.

Your custom, on the other hand, is to refrain if you can from abusive language and outbursts of temper. It's enough that you show your effort to remain silent. Your antagonist will get the idea that further provocation is really asking for trouble. Most daily annoyances are inanimate: the ring of the telephone, the TV screen that goes berserk, the flickering light bulb. Such things prove annoying only if enduring them calls for patience or if attending to them would be a bothersome chore.

Vexation is the state of being annoyed. Its first facial event will involve the lips, usually drawn and sealed, or a twitch in that direction. However, it is not uncommon for the lips to be protruded somewhat firmly, either open or pursed, as in kissing. Any such attitude of lips, where they enter into facial expression, would seem to signal that one is on the verge of speaking out but is making an effort to remain silent. Try right now to look very annoyed. Imagine that your neighbor's child has been spitefully slamming doors for the past five minutes. You would like to wring the little demon's neck, or at least blast at his parents with a few stinging pellets of advice. But you hold your tongue and only hope the next slam will be on the kid's rump. So your lips seal tightly or protrude themselves firmly to withhold that venomous blast. But did you also frown? In Chapter Three, we saw the brow pattern of a frown. Remember the "quotation mark" wrinkles between contracted brows? *Scowl* and *frown* are two words for the same pattern. It is correct to speak of scowling from ill humor or sullenness, whereas frowning more often describes disapproval, annoyance, and anger. But we won't worry too much here about the distinction.

The reason for frowning in vexation was implied when you were on the verge of blasting out at the parents of the door-slamming child. It is just another encounter with the facial preparation for violent expiration. You may even have felt your eyelids become tense and squinted.

Why Ask *Me?*

Before letting this discussion proceed on its logical course into the realm of outright anger, it would be convenient here to look at the face of *helplessness.* Back in Chapter Three came the revelation that you weren't so helpless after all. While you were in the nursery you had your trumpet of displeasure. And in Chapter Four you learned to made do without it. Here your intended response is to appear helpless. This is hardly related emotionally to the face of vexation. Yet helplessness belongs nowhere else in this book, and it does often share the lip pattern of vexation. The reason is not a determination to remain silent but simply a deliberate indication that one has nothing whatsoever to say. And a number of gestures go with this expression, all similarly indicating negation, the lack of information, interest, opinion, or capacity.

Here's a famous quotation: "That's one small step for man, one giant leap for mankind." Do you remember where that was said? Or how about this quotation: "I have nothing to offer but blood, toil, tears, and sweat."

Who said it? And what does it bring to mind? Maybe you couldn't care less. So you shrug your shoulders and draw your elbows in close to your body, you turn your hands palm-side up, fingers separated; your lips stretch out, twist, pucker, or even drop open; your eyebrows rise and fall or draw into a frown. What a symphonic chord you have sounded! And every instrument contributed its own special timbre.

There would seem to be the deliberate effort to dispel every appearance of confident self-assertion and command. In some ways, the shrug of helplessness suggests an effort to pull in one's horns and look a bit smaller and less significant. The fact that the shoulders rise toward the ears might call to mind the way a turtle draws into its shell of security. The upturned palms and separated fingers show that you have nothing to offer. Either tightened or loosely separated lips make it clear you have nothing to say. And if brows are not contracted in a frown, their momentary rise and fall suggest a polite but fleeting effort to comprehend the question and find the answer. But enough of this digression about helplessness. Perhaps the digression itself annoyed you. If so, you are in fine shape now to be provoked further.

Tampering with Tempers

There is a limit to what you can endure calmly under provocation. Let's take thirty seconds to test your capacity to keep a level head. Of course, you must have a watch with a second hand. Alternate counting from 1 to 30 with reciting the alphabet from A to Z. Thus:

$$1 - A - 2 - B - 3 - C - etc.$$

Did you make all the calls correctly, or did you fumble somewhere? If this was too easy, substitute for the dash a person's name:

1 Sally A Tom 2 Bill B Mary 3 John etc.

Did that ruffle you or exasperate you? Who knows? Perhaps you even flew off the handle and hurled this book into the air! That would be a demonstration of temper indeed. But in its indulgence your annoyance would have evaporated.

Anger is an intense displeasure that bears the stamp of antagonism. In general, anger is excited by a sense of wrong, injury, or insult either to oneself or to others. You grow angry if you discover that someone is broadcasting a malicious lie about you or if someone berates you or the things you have done. There is only one anger. Yet we use certain other words to lend special meanings to this state of strong displeasure. *Indignation,* for instance, tells us something about the cause of anger. Whatever has aroused it is looked upon as mean, cruel, or shameful. *Wrath* tells us something about the party who is angered. Here, there is the implication of omnipotence and the might to work vengeance.

Anger, as an emotion, may persist for some length of time at the smouldering level. If this is the case, it cannot necessarily be distinguished from vexation. People talk about holding it in. However, a smouldering anger may be so keenly felt as to speed up the circulation of blood. Thus, an angry person grows hot under the collar. A red flush comes into his or her face, and the eyes brighten (see Chapter Six). There may be a detectable loss of composure in smouldering anger, with the accumulating energy spending itself in meaningless movement (see Chapter One). You must not expect to simulate entirely this level of anger in the absence of a genuine provocation.

The Flare-Up

When anger goes into action, it leaves self-control behind. If anger foams and bubbles, then *rage* boils over with the urge to retaliate. If a person is robbed of a day's earnings, it is that person, not the robber, who is enraged. But when murder is committed from a passion of anger, the killer is enraged to the point of madness. His highly dangerous emotion is called *fury.* Here, in full dress, are all the ominous features of hostility. Here is the terrible violence at which the less active forms of vexation and anger only hinted. Now, instead of idly threatening to wring a neck, the enraged man will be swept forward in a tidal wave of blind fury until his heinous revenge has been wreaked.

Not all violent crime springs from rage—perhaps a comparatively small part. We must not concern ourselves with the abundance of hoodlum violence. Evidently, violence for thrills is a very different matter.

Take a look in your mirror, and pretend to yourself that this person before you has aroused your anger by brutally kicking the dog that trotted faithfully at his side. Or he might have viciously slapped a defenseless young child. Are you steamed up? See what your upper lip is doing. You'll find it's not unlike the upper-lip retraction of disgust. The chief difference is the searing stare of your eyes. With lowered brows, you glower at this loathesome person. And your jaw drops open in a gasp (see Chapter Eight). As long as the lip curls up around the wings

SNARL

SNEER

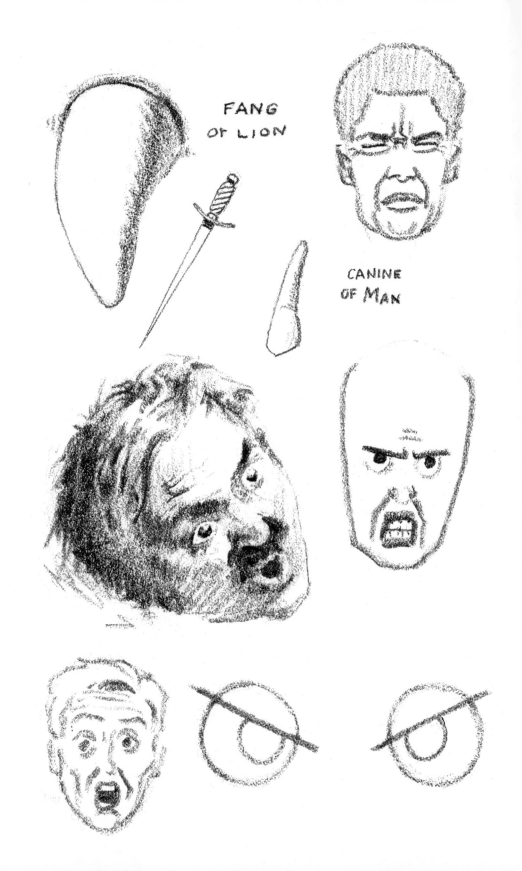

FANG OF LION

CANINE OF MAN

of the nose on both sides, the element of disgust is present. But you may, instead, feel a twitch of the raised lip off to one side only. This is the very special emblem of hostility.

Snarling

A snarl draws one end of the upper lip upward and outward toward the eye of the same side. Muscles that raise this curtain of flesh pull from an anchorage just below the eye and deepen the natural furrow that runs from wing of nose to corner of mouth. A secondary effect is to pucker the lower eyelid and push it slightly upward on the eye. A restrained snarl can be shown with the lips closed. But an openly vicious snarl separates both lips at one end to display both upper and lower canine teeth. This is all you have in the way of fangs.

In the animal world, an exceptionally big canine tooth is the badge of flesh-eating (carnivorous) creatures. Its daggerlike stab is useful for puncturing and tearing into live prey. It is thus an important weapon in combat, whether offensive or defensive. You, at gunpoint, would not wait to see the trigger pulled before feeling overpowered. The mere sight of a lethal weapon can be an effective threat. The snarl of a predatory animal is just as threatening. It is readying, as it were, for the first stab. The adversary, seeing the terrible fangs, will very likely be warded off. It's like a sign that reads "Danger—Sharp Points Ahead—Proceed at Your Own Risk!" So a snarl is a relic from the dim, prehistoric past, inherited from our early forebears. Whereas the once impressive canine teeth have now dwindled to short, blunt stumps, a human ability to display them in hostility has been perpetuated even to the twentieth century. A genuine snarl by modern man may seem a bit ridiculous, but it should not be regarded lightly. Modern man still bites. And when he snarls in earnest, we can hear him growling: "Danger—Don't Push Your Luck!"

Most of us favor one side or the other for snarling. And you may find you can't snarl at all with a particular side of your mouth. Yet, under provocation, it's instinctive to use the side toward your offender. If he or she is to the left, you're apt to snarl left.

Some animals bare all their front teeth when they feel hostile. People do this too. By retraction of both lips we can display the whole arsenal, so to speak. The one-sided snarl is used slyly as a warning; the full arsenal of teeth is more forthright and is likely to be flashed at the instant of attack.

The Wide-Open Throttle

If you come face to face with a threatening opponent, you must make a choice: fight or flight. This chapter deals with getting you ready to fight—the preparation for combat. And what may ensue is a life-or-death struggle to the finish. This is a highly physiological matter. There are many details to be attended to. But Mother Nature has taken care of everything. Two small adrenal glands are perched like dunce caps atop the kidneys. In a dangerous situation, the brain orders these glands to secrete their hormones. And the secretion works miracles throughout your body. One of the hormones, adrenaline, causes you to breathe more deeply, your heart to beat faster, and your blood pressure to rise. Rage is surely not sweet to contemplate, yet sugar is released in quantity to the blood—destination muscle. How well you know the value of sugar as a quick source of energy for weary arms and legs. And this shot of adrenaline makes it possible for your blood to coagulate more rapidly than usual. Do you see how farsighted Mother Nature was in her provisions for emergency? Another hormone, noradrenaline, is also secreted by these same glands. As a result, the small blood vessels tend to contract and resist the flow of blood. This would seem to be a further provision for your survival in the event of open wounds and hemorrhage. In every respect you are primed to do battle. You are given a fighting chance to see it through—perhaps as victor.

The facial exhibit of this complicated preparation is mostly the high color of skin we mentioned before. Eyes may be bright, but they may also go bloodshot. You see red. One detail is related to the deeper and faster breathing. You must have oxygen—loads of oxygen in your blood. So your mouth drops open to gulp down air in greater volume. An instinctive pattern will be the dilated nostrils. You can dilate your nostrils at will with the face in repose. Yet, if you so much as raise your upper lip to display your teeth, the nostrils will flare open in spite of you. At this point, it should be perfectly clear that you needn't worry about your ability to be ferocious if you are provoked. It comes quite naturally.

Overdoing It

After all this discussion of angry behavior, you are still due for a surprise feature. It's a good bet that you've never been aware of it. At first glance, the matter seems too trivial to bother with at all and too silly to take seriously. Yet it's there, and it has a history. And, of all things, it happens to be the ears!

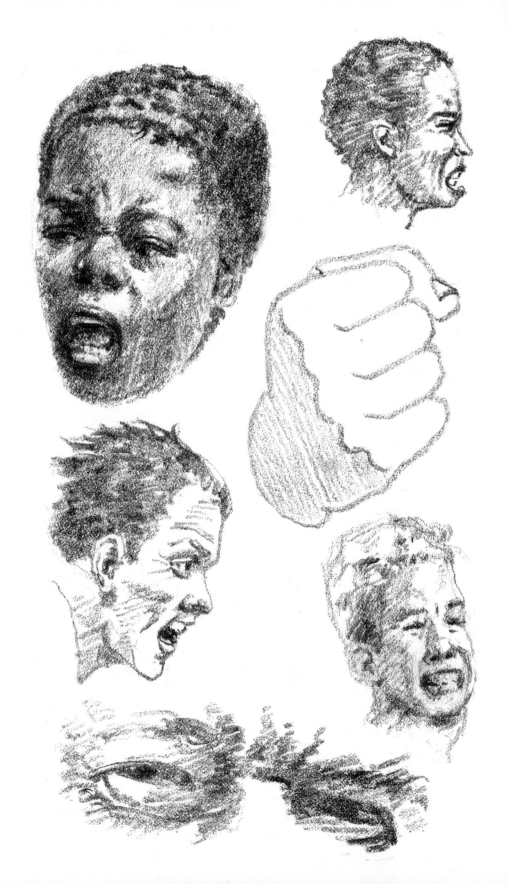

During a fit of rage, the ears may draw backward and close to the head. Yes, this is the very same movement you perform at will if you can wiggle your ears. The matter was mentioned briefly in Chapter Two. The sensation is one of tightening the flesh around the ears. What takes place is the contraction of a thin ribbon of muscle fibers attaching to the ear from behind. Such a contraction will draw the ear backward and the top of it in toward the head; the lobe will move slightly outward away from the head. You can watch part of this happen in your mirror. Some people find they must tighten the whole scalp in order to wiggle their ears, because the scalp and ear muscles are inclined to contract together. There is also a band of muscle in front of the ear that can draw the ear forward. But the individual who can voluntarily move ears forward is rare.

Most likely, you have already hit upon the significance of flattening the ears backward in a fit of rage. An animal with big, long ears knows by instinct what an easy mark they are for its opponent. So, also by instinct, such an animal will retract its ears in combat to prevent them from being cruelly clawed or bitten.

Fortunately, our legacy from our primitive ancestors does not include large, vulnerable ears. It's as if prominent ears went out of fashion. They must have shrunk and dwindled down through the ages—until what ears we have are small and nearly flat against the head. Yet, for no special reason, the muscles to work the ears have lingered on, degenerating at a slower rate. So useless are these ear muscles to Homo Sapiens that they have almost forgotten how to contract. Even with H. Sapiens' nearest relatives, the gorilla and the chimpanzee, there is scarcely any greater ability to move the ears. One must look to a more distant primate relative, the little ratlike tarsier, for mobile ears. They are enormous too. Mobility is an advantage in orienting the hollow shell of the ear so that it may collect sound waves from various directions. And collecting sound waves can be mighty important if you're a little tarsier springing among the branches all night. Big ears are fine collectors and detectors, but they're painfully vulnerable. So their mobility serves in another way to help them seek safety close against the head.

Because we share with many animals the muscular equipment for ear retraction, and because so many animals can be seen to exhibit this movement in rage, it seems quite possible that we share also the tendency to twitch the ears backward in rage. You will not need your mirror to test this. The sensation of tightness around your ears will tell you. But you must first simulate rage. And a good way to start is by learning to mutter aloud, "You dirty rat!"

In what appears to be the coming age of interplanetary ballistics, the weapons of warfare will surely disown the lowly bayonet. Drill sergeants will no longer face the problem of how to incite a passion of rage in bayonet drill. Their howling of foul oaths and bestial obscenities will be heard no more. Perhaps rage itself will sometime vanish in a more civilized and godly world. Perhaps the dictionaries of the future will politely list such words as *rage* and *fury* and simply affix the notation "Obs."

CHAPTER ELEVEN

FROZEN SPINES

Scared?

Do you have any qualms about striking a match? Ordinarily no, you say, except near gasoline or some other volatile or highly combustible substance that would start a conflagration. In other words, you are not afraid of fire as such, but of the danger created by attending hazards. The instant that uncontrollable danger is perceived will usually mark the beginning of fear.

A car is a potential weapon of death and destruction. Yet you surely don't suffer fear every second of your driving time. Automatically, you are calculating the danger of rough embankments and steep ditches at the sides of highways, the degree of centrifugal force at curves, the danger of meeting other cars, passing other cars, or trailing them. But you drive in confidence—as long as you feel you have control. Let just one unexpected danger, such as the careening approach of an erratic driver, suddenly loom into your peaceful calculations, and you realize that you are no longer master of the situation. You do the best you can. When the emergency is past, perhaps you notice your sweaty palms or a thumping in your chest. Fear results from an awareness of imminent danger to oneself or others, combined with an awareness of insufficient control or power to circumvent the danger.

What is looked upon as dangerous by one person may not be so considered by another. A little child may be afraid of thunder. A father may be more afraid of losing a business account. And a grandfather may be more afraid of slipping on an icy pavement. But in each case there is apparent threat and the insecure feeling of lacking control.

Severe bodily injury is one of the most potent objects of fear and embraces many "subfears": the fear of falling, the fear of strange animals, the fear of lightning, fire, darkness, and firearms. There are, of course, those stalwart individuals who can face the threat of severe bodily injury without apparent agitation. Yet one threat in particular will reduce even the most stout-hearted to quaking. That is the threat of asphyxiation. Whereas a human life can persist for days without sleep, food, or water, it can survive only a matter of minutes without air.

The causes of fear are not limited to grim threats to one's physical well-being. The prospect of ridicule, for instance, can strike fear into people's hearts. And it's common to fear disgrace, rejection, and reprimand—society's challenges to one's worth or reputation. Somewhere in this area lies the notorious affliction called stage fright.

In ancient Greek mythology, Ares was the counterpart of Mars, the god of war. And Ares had two sons, Deimos and Phobos, who prepared his war chariot for battle. Astronomers see Deimos and Phobos in the sky at night as tiny satellites of the planet Mars. Odd that the god of war and battle should name his sons "Panic" and "Fear"! The Greek word *phobos* means fear. Hence the list of phobias that beset modern man. In our language, phobia implies a special kind of fear—unreasonable in that it is firmly established as a conditioned response. Unreasonable fears can be just as unnerving as reasonable fears. But one who is afraid to cross the street simply because he is afraid to cross any street, that fellow harbors an unreasonable fear. This phobia is intensely felt. And it may possibly be detected in the person's face or behavior. One source lists about a hundred varieties of phobias. Even the person who fears just about everything has a "panophobia." And if he has a fear of his own fears, psychologists call that a "phobophobia." So everything and everybody is covered, including the psychologists. With phobias, the perception of danger, threat, or intense repugnance may have so little foundation as to seem absurd. And the sufferer, recognizing its absurdity, usually struggles valiantly and in silence to conceal the fear that disarms him. Perhaps another person in his company takes notice only that the poor fellow has gone pale. The curse of a phobia is not only its unreasonableness but also its inevitability. It is painfully predictable.

Watch Your Language!

Anyone who speaks a language at all can string together the words that give a sentence its basic thought. Thus: Ted opened the door and looked in. This is sheer statement of fact and tells us nothing of how Ted opened and how he looked. We can imagine him breaking down the door by

brute force, or prying it into little pieces with a crowbar, or stealthily lifting the latch, or merrily flinging the door wide on its hinges. There are many ways to open a door, and many ways to look in.

Most of us find that our conversational vocabulary is wanting in vividness. Unable to summon the word that will precisely suggest a quality, we resort to crude exaggeration. Hence the overworked and usually inappropriate adjectives of conversation:

fabulous	terrific	stunning
incredible	stupendous	agonizing
terrible	wonderful	marvelous
horrible	beautiful	excruciating
sensational	colossal	fantastic

And dozens of others. Such words bandied about have little meaning. It is unfortunate that among the conversational adjectives are found the words you and I must now use discreetly: *fearful, dreadful, alarming, frightening, terrifying,* and *horrifying.*

Fear is a very general term. It is the disturbed state of feeling aroused by forebodings of coming misfortune or danger. The nervous apprehension of a mother who sees her baby reach for a pair of scissors is a mild form of fear. *Dread* is much like fear but denotes a more overwhelming apprehension. Some people live with a constant dread of disease. *Alarm* is a fear excited in the face of a sudden or unexpected threat. It is thus an agitation mingled with wide-eyed surprise. One has cause for alarm who wakes up to find himself sprawled across a railroad track. *Fright* is similar to alarm but implies short duration, sometimes a trifling cause. A person can suffer fright upon being startled by a swerving car on the road or by an unexpected tap on the shoulder from behind. *Terror* is an extreme fear that prostrates and confuses one's faculties, especially when the fearful thing is formidable and inevitable. Both power and violence combine to arouse terror in the weak or defenseless. Villagers may cower in terror as the conquering army rolls through their streets in an orgy of plunder and desecration.

Horror adds the special quality of repugnance or loathing to what is also fearful. We speak of the horrors of war, having in mind the cruelties that are inflicted and the atrocities that are committed. Some years ago, a sickening horror was struck in the hearts of many people when they learned about a dog that was buried alive by two drunken men. Those men were punished with substantial prison terms, but even that was a mercy such brutes could not appreciate.

Fear, dread, and terror are really stages in a progression from apprehension to complete prostration. In all but the final stage before collapse, there is likely to be some trace of the trouble pattern: oblique eyebrows and a puckering of skin at the center of the forehead (see Chapter Four). Alarm and fright introduce the element of surprise—what is sudden or unexpected. So they draw the brows high on the head and raise the upper eyelids, causing the eyes almost to start from their sockets. The jaw gapes, allowing the open mouth to gasp and to utter a shout or scream. Horror is a special variety of fearfulness. It amounts to a vile assault upon one's sensibilities, arousing the extremest kind of revulsion. Add to the intensity of terror a raised upper lip and perhaps a tongue protruded upon the lower lip (see Chapter Nine), and we have the facial pattern of horror.

Tightening the Harp Strings

If your mirror has been getting cold, here's a chance to warm it up. Watch what happens now as you perform. Separate your lips loosely, clench your teeth firmly, and then make your lower lip drop very slightly toward your chin. It can't go far, but it will bare your lower front teeth. Hold this position of lip separation, and place a hand loosely around the front and side of your neck. Now, stretch the corners of your mouth outward as if you were trying to exhibit all the lower teeth in the back of your mouth. If you do this energetically with all the force you can muster, your hand will probably feel a tightening of skin at the front and side of your neck. Now drop your hand, and repeat the tension so you can watch it in the mirror. If this thin, sheetlike muscle in your neck and shoulders is well developed, you will see its fibrous strands rise up taut under the skin—like the strings on a harp. The muscle fibers sweep upward on either side from the region of your collarbone to converge on a small area around the corner of your mouth. When they contract, they draw the corner of the mouth outward and downward. But they usually contract only in strenuous situations when other mouth muscles have become fatigued. Thus, these fibers seem to be a kind of last resort. You will notice these harp strings in the newsphoto of runners coming up to the finish line of a race. Muscles that ordinarily hold the mouth spread wide (for greater intake of air) may be failing, so the thin sheet of harp-string fibers helps out. This neck muscle is brought into play in many kinds of physical exertion where a wide-open mouth is not actually needed, as in violent but momentary pulling, pushing, ripping, hurling, pounding, and so on. So there is some question as to how much this muscle acts as a last resort and how much out of sheer empathy (see Chapter Two).

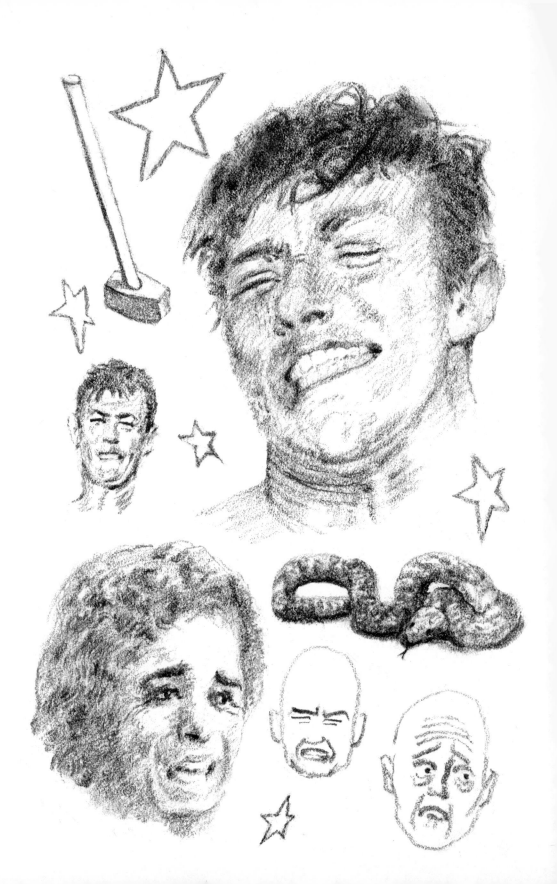

After all these words about the harp-string muscle under the skin of the neck, it seems almost unkind to suggest that it may or may not jump up in extreme terror and horror. Certainly, it tightens during a violent scream. And it has even been nicknamed the fright muscle. But it does seem doubtful that this flimsy sheet of fibers would ever remain contracted long enough to be recognized as a regular feature of the pattern of terror or horror. Whatever its status, let us admit that its presence, though fleeting, can add violence to what is already pitifully intense.

Flight

In Chapter Ten, it was mentioned that a threat must be dealt with by fight or flight. And that chapter was concerned with meeting danger head on—the preparation for combat. In this chapter we are talking about threats over which we have no control. We have no choice but to resort to the alternative of flight, if that is possible.

Nearly all creatures of the Earth are equipped in some way to dodge their more powerful pursuers. Although some rely on cunning and deception, most animals just retreat in haste: the mouse scampers from the cat, the chicken from the hawk, the gazelle from the lion. For human beings, flight means running. Our chances of survival may depend solely upon how fast and how far we can run. Exploring this idea may shed light on the subject of fear.

Running, whether in sport or in panic, can be as energetic as any combat. The demands made by extreme muscular exertion—rapid circulation and breathing—take priority. The heart doubles its blood-pumping schedule and seems to pound against the breastbone. The chest abandons the casual rise and fall of ordinary breathing to accelerate the cycle of respiration. The mouth drops open and the nostrils flare to expedite the intake of air. At the same time, the open mouth permits more silent breathing. It may happen that silence and concealment will play an important part in the retreat. *Perspiration* is also stepped up, especially copious on the palms of the hands and soles of the feet. Moisture here would seem to allow for better grip and traction in making a getaway, if you think of a person as a naked animal eluding some swift enemy in pursuit. We have already taken note of the cooling function of perspiration when body heat is increased. So the face too may break out with beads of sweat. This much of the preparation for flight is very like that for combat. And these provisions for emergency struggle or flight are looked out for by the autonomic nervous system. So they are processes over which we have no control.

On the other hand, running—even crawling—may be impossible. If our fear is overmastering, we may be totally immobilized. Our muscles may go into convulsions of trembling. Chattering of the teeth is, of course, the result of tremor in the jaw muscles. A further extreme is the total collapse of strength when muscles turn to jelly. Muscular performance of legs and arms is brought about through the central nervous system and is a process usually subject to our voluntary control. Apparently, the Creator figured it was sufficient to provide us with a special reserve of power for emergency, and that we should at least be sensible enough to use it!

White as a Sheet

Not all human flight takes to a pair of legs. Civilized man, in fact, rarely encounters the kind of threat where actual leg speed will be his salvation. For most of us, gone are the days of being surrounded by packs of hungry wild animals. And a very small part of the Earth's population lives at the feet of active volcanoes. But fears we have, just the same. Instead of savage animals, we must cope with reckless drivers. Instead of bubbling volcanoes, we must deal with space-age missiles. A respectable pair of legs is nowadays little more than a social asset at the beach.

In an overmastering fear, one seems to be saying to oneself, "If only there were some escape from this dreadful situation! If only I could just vanish from it!" The eyes are widely opened and roll restlessly in their sockets, as if to search for a possible escape route. And there is a contraction of the small blood vessels under the skin, driving the circulated blood deeper into the body. In quite a literal way, one is automatically shrinking into oneself—hiding, as it were, beneath one's own skin. And that skin, drained of its blood, goes white. You will know what this looks like if you've watched your own fingers go white from exposure to intense cold. As a matter of fact, the reduced blood supply means a reduced supply of heat and impaired sensitivity. Blanched skin will be both cooler to the touch and numb. Since the skin grows not only pallid and cool but also moist with profuse sweating, we have in fear the very special condition of pale, clammy skin. Hence, the expression "cold sweat."

Thrills

What sort of thing really "sends" you? A ride on a roller coaster? A good Western thriller? Beethoven's Ninth? A day at the World Series? The bejewelled void of the heavens on a clear night? The sight of trailing arbu-

SHIVERING FROM CHILL.

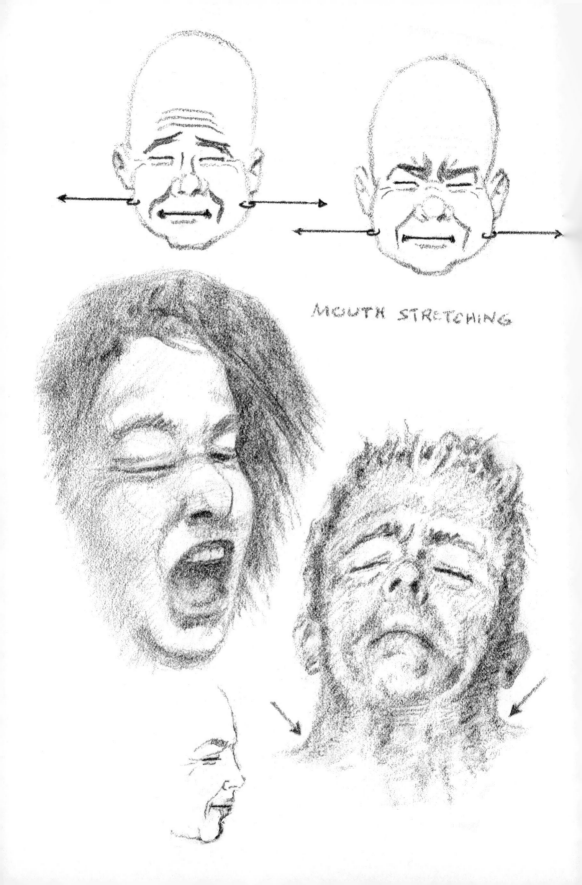

MOUTH STRETCHING

tus in the woods at springtime? Or a view from the top of the Eiffel Tower? All such things can provide thrills. We are inclined to think of a thrill as nothing more specific than great excitement. Actually, *thrill* means simply a tingling, trembling, or shivering—no matter what the cause. Being very correct about this, you must admit that real thrills of emotion are not everyday experiences.

The shudder of fright is a thrill caused by the same phenomenon as the shudder or shiver of sudden chill. In both cases, the surface of the body has been rapidly depleted of its blood. If your own fingers have gone white and numb, as we said, from exposure to intense cold, most likely you have worked those fingers until warmth and sensation returned to them. It would seem that a shudder of the shoulders is a reflex pattern to similarly activate muscles in the chilled upper torso, thereby stimulating the flow of blood.

Shivering of the entire body may accompany any of the overpowering emotions. Less extensive and far more common is the momentary chilling of the spine. It is interesting that perfectly harmless things, even pleasurable things, can produce a shiver as much as any fright. But one must perceive in the thrilling stimulus a might or majesty or perfection so imposing as to render one utterly powerless or insignificant. The feeling of devastation is usually at the subconscious level.

Momentous occasions are always potential thrillers. They may be of historic nature, such as coronations and rocket firings into outer space. Or the momentous occasion may be personal, such as receiving one's high school diploma or glimpsing the first sight of land after a long voyage at sea. A shiver will be in order on any of these occasions, just because they are thrilling.

An event that captured the attention and imagination of almost the whole human race at one and the same instant was the historic moon landing at 4:17:43 P.M., E.D.T., July 20, 1969. It was a thrill greater by far than a mighty military procession—because there was also the element of reverential awe and mystery.

Shy of Saliva

A classic feature of fear, though not visible in itself, is the drying of the mouth. Normally, the salivary glands pour their watery secretions into the mouth and maintain its moistness. Every twenty-four hours they secrete something like a quart of saliva. This naturally leads to an occasional swallow for evacuation of the accumulating secretions. Thus, the linings of both mouth and throat are kept constantly moist. Saliva has a cleansing and buffering effect and helps to prevent food particles from lodging and promoting the growth of bacteria. But it also lubricates the mouth for the passage of dry foods and for the articulation of speech.

Saliva is about 99½ percent water and is subject to any general dehydration. So the secretion is suppressed whenever there is a loss of body fluid. And certainly in fear the loss through perspiration is notorious. A common accompaniment of the cold sweat of fear, then, is dryness of the mouth and throat. This is something we can't see; only the frightened subject can feel it. But we do see his pitiful gagging attempts to swallow saliva that just isn't there!

If you try to swallow five or six times in succession, you will become aware of the increasing difficulty. It is letting saliva run to the back of the tongue that helps you start the swallow reflex. Naturally, successive gulps will clear the mouth of saliva and make increasingly difficult any effort to start the reflex. But notice this about your swallowing. There are two stages of the process that you can identify if you observe carefully. First, you voluntarily push the tongue up against the roof of your mouth. This is followed by certain muscular contractions at the back of the throat. You will be vaguely aware of them too. The second stage is a quick rise and fall of your larynx. We described this in Chapter Three as including the prominent throat bump called the Adam's apple. You can watch this take place in your mirror, or you can follow the course of the Adam's apple with your finger tip. Just one more thing: do you find yourself lowering your chin slightly toward your chest when swallowing becomes difficult? A high lift of the chin puts tension on the larynx, allowing it little play. And this inhibits swallowing. When the chin is lowered a very little bit from its natural level, the larynx is given greater freedom. This gagging attempt to swallow can sometimes be one of the few visible signs of overwhelming fear. Speech, if it comes at all, will be thin and rasping at best. Earlier, the face may have prepared itself gallantly to utter the piercing scream of distress (see Chapter Three), but any utterance now is likely to be a tremulous and ineffectual squawk.

A Hair-Raising Experiment

Your picture of fear is not complete without one final touch: the bristling of hair. But it must be understood right away that hair raising is not alone a feature of fear. It may accompany rage too (see Chapter Ten), as well as the ordinary chill.

A simple experiment will illustrate what happens. But you must have a long pencil at hand. Anything such as a pipe cleaner will work, as long

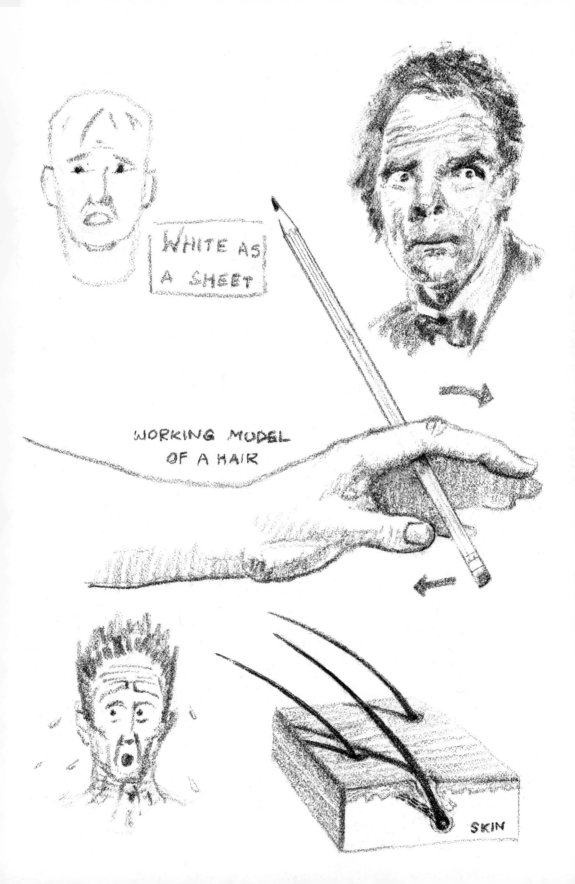

WHITE AS
A SHEET

WORKING MODEL
OF A HAIR

SKIN

as it is long and slim like a human hair. Hold one hand, palm downward, out in front of you so that the thumbnail faces you. Take the pencil in your other hand (with its point upward) and slide it as far as possible between middle and ring fingers, so that it comes to lie obliquely against the webbing between those fingers. The slant will be about forty-five degrees. No more than one inch of the pencil should appear below the hand. Now imagine that the back of your hand is the magnified skin surface of some part of your body. Let the pencil represent a human hair lying back, as it would, at an angle to the surface. You can even pretend to brush it smoothly backward with the other hand. The lower inch of the pencil beneath your hand is the root of the hair. Here is a working model that will explain the hair-raising mechanism.

All you have to do to make the model work is reach under with the thumb and pull backward on the lower inch of the pencil. In true lever fashion, this causes the rest of the pencil to swing in the forward direction. Your thumb has played the role of a very tiny muscle that attaches to a hair root from behind. When contracted, it tugs on the hair root and rocks the hair into an upright position. The natural hair follicle (sac containing the hair root) lies at an angle below the skin, just as your model indicated before it started working. So when the tiny hair muscle relaxes, the hair is allowed to drop back to its original slope. Obviously, then, it is these tiny muscles at the roots of your hairs that may go into contraction during a chill or when you experience a sudden fright.

One embellishment of the hair-raising process is the small hump that rises on the skin where the hair grows out. You call the knobby surface goose flesh. Since the tiny hair muscle slants downward behind the hair root to which it attaches, a contraction will draw the hair root upward as well as backward. The effect is to make the visible hair rise as well as rock upward. And, as the hair rises, a portion of the skin surrounding it at the surface will be dragged upward along with the hair. And this is the knob of goose flesh.

Perhaps you have noticed that you can't have goose flesh where there is no hair, such as on the palms of your hands. Bristling of hair will always be accompanied by goose flesh, whether it is caused by chill, thrill, rage, or fright. Surely, it is in order now to ask why the tiny hair muscles exist at all. What can be the advantage of bristling the hair?

Hairy Heat Control

It is generally believed that the very early progenitors of man were abundantly supplied with hair over most of the body surface. Man, as you know, belongs to the class of mammals. And one characteristic of mammals is that they have hair. At the beach today, one sees occasional evidence that modern man can still sprout an almost beastlike bounty of hair. Some people consider this hairiness unsightly. On the other hand, a mass of well-groomed hair on a woman's head is looked upon with pleasure, her crowning glory. Yet, to be very practical about it, the function of hair is to help regulate body temperature by insulating the skin against loss of body heat. In cold weather, the little hair muscles contract to lift up the covering of hair. This increases the insulation space between hair and skin and retards the escape of heat. Birds ruffle their feathers in cold weather for the same reason. In warm weather, hair lies close to the surface to decrease its insulating effect.

Have you noticed how the hairs on your forearm stand up high when you feel chilly? And the goose flesh too, of course. A sudden and pronounced chill may cause a tingling sensation to run through your entire scalp and down your shoulders and spine. You can't see what is happening, but this sensation is produced by body hair rising up on cold skin.

If you have ever seen an angry dog or cat, you may have noticed a ruffling of the hair. Darwin suggested this was probably a defense mechanism of rage—to make the animal look larger and more ferocious in the eyes of its adversary and so to ward off further aggression. But, here again, Darwin is endowing the animal with the capacity to employ a mechanism spontaneously as a signal. Furthermore, it seems doubtful that an animal can appreciate a change in its own apparent size sufficiently to utilize the mechanism for impressing a foe. First of all, I suspect that we interpret the bristling of an animal's hair as a sign of ferocity only because it makes the animal larger and more ferocious in our own human eyes. We cannot be sure it is this particular feature that intimidates other animals. Certainly, it can be observed among breeds of dogs that the large size of one animal does not necessarily bestow fearlessness upon him and imbue a smaller animal with intimidation.

Certain creatures, it is true, are endowed with defense mechanisms that make them momentarily larger and more formidable. The globe fish (balloon fish or puffer) is an example. It has no scales, but rather a skin covered with prickly spines. By swallowing air or water it distends itself to a large round ball and the spines stand out menacingly. At the same time, it rolls belly upward, floating to the surface where it bobs along with the waves. The increased size and the thorny armor make the inflated globe fish too big a mouthful for some of the larger fish. And perhaps it is doing them a favor, for the flesh of the globe fish can be highly poisonous. But the special endowment of inflatability would seem to be the poor fish's only mechanism of defense.

Since a mammal's coat of hair does have its own physiological function to perform, this raises the question of how the animal can discover the incidental and rather minor ballooning effect of raising its hair. Since the function of bristling is very evidently a factor in heat control, it suggests that some need of heat control may exist in the extreme emotional state of fright and the related phenomenon of thrill. We have already discussed the cold trepidations of fright and a spine-chilling shiver in situations where one is rendered powerless or insignificant by overwhelmingly impressive elements. There can be no difficulty, then, in accepting the matter of surface cooling (due to contraction of surface blood vessels) as sufficient excuse for hair raising in similar emotional states. It leaves only to account for bristling in the emotional state of rage.

To be consistent, we must suspect that in rage also cooling of the skin—even momentary—takes place just prior to bristling. So we face a rather peculiar picture. Rage, which is looked upon as quite the opposite of fear, apparently may be complicated by a trace of fearful feelings. Unless the enraged person flies instantly into full-scale combat, which he rarely does, it seems entirely plausible that he first takes stock of the dangers involved. And taking stock of danger has been the subject of this whole chapter!

CHAPTER TWELVE

QUICK,
THE MORPHINE!

Red Light

I applaud your courage in persevering this far. This last chapter is not
the happy ending you deserve. But the plan is quite deliberate. If you
are exhausted, you are in excellent shape for some remarks about pain!
Regarding the ingredients of facial expression, we have already covered
them. Only a few oddments are left to pick over. Yet we would be re-
miss not to probe this final sphere of unpleasantness. So let us consider
the nature of pain and what it does for the sufferer.

Possibly you stopped in your tracks at the idea of pain doing anything
for the sufferer. Nothing could be more obvious than the curse of pain.
But pain is a red light, a warning signal that can sometimes prevent further and more serious injury. The prick of a finger causes the finger to
be withdrawn—and fast! Without painful sensation, it is conceivable
there might be loss of limb, even loss of life. It's the toothache that hur-
ries one to the dentist, the corn on a toe that makes one look for better-
fitting shoes, the burnt tongue that advises against swallowing overheated
food. Not all pains can be so easily tracked down as warning signals. But
there is little doubt that by commanding attention the sensation of pain
compels one to desist from what he or she is doing or to enter upon some
course of remedial action.

Pain has personality. It can exist as a momentary twinge or a sustained
ache, or it can be recurring. And there are several varieties of pain. Your
physician not only wants to know where the sensation is located but also

wants you to describe its character. This helps to determine the cause of pain. So you cast about in your mind for the appropriate word:

sharp	stabbing	searing	grinding
dull	darting	racking	piercing
aching	shooting	stinging	burning
throbbing			

Or maybe you come up with a still more vivid adjective.

The most important aspect of pain is its severity. The range of unpleasant sensation is from the most trifling uneasiness (moderate hunger) to the most agonizing torture. Just where we begin to call it pain is up to us. What we consider as our pain threshold is a matter of how stoical we are. Needless to say, some of us groan and carry on with the slightest discomfort. Others endure far greater suffering without a whimper. The physician is much concerned, of course, with the severity of pain but accepts the patient's evaluation of severity in terms of what he or she already knows about the patient. What Miss Twiddlethumb describes as excruciating pain may be no worse than what Mr. Ironsides calls a little soreness. This varying tolerance of pain sometimes makes it difficult for a doctor to gauge severity with any accuracy. But if the doctor knows Miss Twiddlethumb's history, he or she may decide that a sugar pill will relieve her of the "excruciating" pain. With Mr. Ironsides, the doctor may suspect that the "soreness" calls for penetrating examination, perhaps elaborate tests.

The pill prescribed for Miss Twiddlethumb would be classified as a placebo, but its beneficial effect would be ruined if her doctor were to let her in on the secret. A placebo is a medicine given more to please than benefit the patient. A tincture of gentian compound with peppermint water was a placebo often used in the past. Today, placebos are more often truly medicinal but relatively inactive. What is so interesting about the placebo administered for relief of pain is that it so often works.

In a scientific experiment some years ago, carried out with over 150 patients suffering pain after surgical operations, the patients received injections whenever they asked for something to relieve pain. Sometimes they were given morphine, other times a placebo. The investigators found that more than half of the patients reacted to the placebo, claiming significant relief. This interesting test leads one to suspect that the very ritual of injection and the subsequent contemplation of it may promote relief by distracting the patient's mind. Of course, a more potent factor is the suggestibility of the patient. Some of us just assume that a prescribed dose of medicine will take effect. Others, more skeptical, simply wait and see. But there seems to be substantial evidence that awareness of pain can usually be diminished somewhat by a preoccupation with other things. The man with a lame knee may forget his ailment altogether in the face of greater affliction, such as acute financial reverses. Very shortly, we shall see how the body seems to engage itself in distraction of its own creation.

Action!

A physician would say that pain is an impression on a sensory nerve causing distress. A psychologist might say that pain is a form of consciousness characterized by desire for escape or avoidance. Our point of view here is something like a combination of the two. Let's say that pain is an impression on a sensory nerve that causes distress and leads to motor response. Since we had quite a tussle with distress in Chapter Four, there is no need to go through it again in detail. If you try squealing "Ouch!" with gusto, you may find that your brows contract suddenly in a synchronized scowl (see Chapter Three). If the sensation of pain is intense, the mouth is opened partway and its corners are pulled back violently toward the ears. This is the familiar "grin" of suffering. The mouth retraction, especially if corners are drawn downward, usually involves a tightening of that "harp string" neck muscle we described in Chapter Eleven. As with great fright, there is apt to be pallor of the skin and a cold sweat. Possible elaborations are the muscular tremblings and the bristling of hairs. As for any set facial or body pattern of distress, these few remarks give the total picture. But notice that this is a set pattern. Our definition of pain declared that the distress leads to motor response. In Chapter Five, we discussed anguish and how much it resembled physical suffering. And we noted that suffering is very largely a motion picture. Throughout the other chapters of this book, we have steered our way carefully through facial expression, avoiding wherever possible the factors of body stance and gesture. They have their own fascinating stories, but they are more generally understood, and their effects are mostly those of reinforcing what is already written in the face. With pain it is different. The behavior of the whole body may be involved.

A painful stimulus provokes immediate motor response—in other words, action. That, unfortunately, explains the merciless whipping of a dray horse (or spurring of a saddle horse) in the days before humane societies kept their vigil to protect dumb animals from cruelty. The human re-

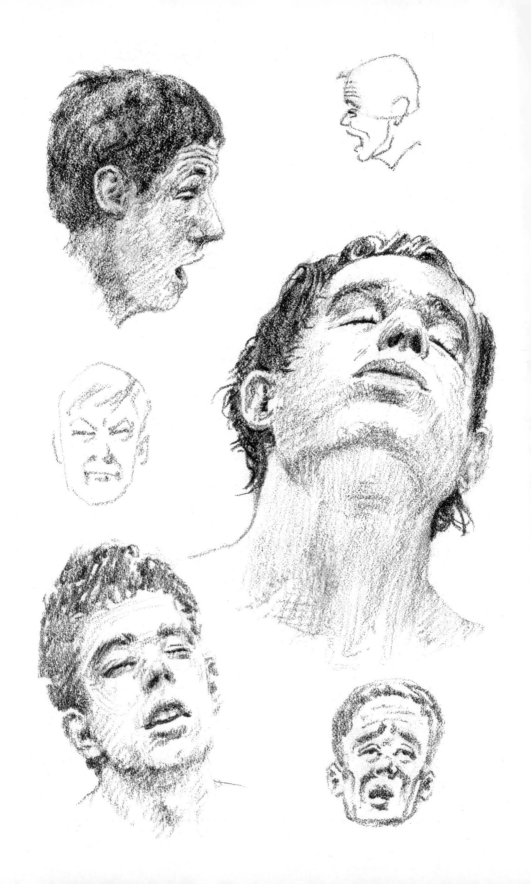

sponse to pain can even approach dancing in its incessant, writhing body movement.

We have already mentioned that you would work your fingers if they went white and numb from exposure to intense cold. This working is a voluntary motor response to an unpleasant sensation. But now, let's say you pinched your finger when closing a cabinet drawer. The finger is withdrawn hastily, and you scowl and wave it for a bit. This also is a motor response. Waving a pinched finger does the finger no particular good. Perhaps it is a subconscious effort to shake off the painful sensation, as if it were a loathsome spider. At any rate, the activity is an outlet for the sudden spurt of energy to do something about the hurt. This variety of pain has surely cropped up in your experience. So the finger waving must already be familiar to you.

Now, going to the extremity of pain, imagine that your fingers are caught and badly squeezed in some infernal machine. Any attempt to extricate the fingers sends a flash of unbearable pain through your arm. Yet what seems equally unbearable is the crushing pain of those imprisoned fingers. Until help arrives, how can you expend the fast-mounting nervous energy of motor response? It is writhing and twisting and flailing movements that help to dissipate the energy. So all but your immobilized arm goes to work. With the free arm, fingers are alternately straightened out and clenched up tight. Even the toes may do this. In the face, the far-stretching grin of suffering is energetically employed. If you are one of much grit, your lips may be sealed against crying out. Otherwise, teeth will be bared somewhat by the parted lips. Even the eyeballs will share in the general excitement, turning in their sockets, partly to scan the environment for help or escape but partly to expend energy.

Have a Bite?

Offhand, it may appear that we have exhausted the possibilities of muscular response. But there is one more region to activate. The clenching of teeth is produced by jaw muscles. So a contraction of these muscles will offer still another outlet for motor response. In view of this, the practice of dentistry probably has its hazards!

A friend of mine who worked with a traveling animal show was once called upon to dress the wound of a Chacma baboon whose forearm had been torn open by an animal in the adjoining cage. The gaping wound required a few stitches, yet the baboon endured bravely and quietly as the needle went in and out. It seemed to understand entirely that this man was helping, not harming. Its only apparent release of energy was the most gentle, guarded sinking of teeth into my friend's shoulder!

Well known is the need to bite on something when one has no choice but to endure extreme pain. In the days when brutal flogging was customary punishment for sailors at sea, the wrists and ankles were tightly bound with thongs to the whipping post. This, of course, was done to prevent escape. But it also greatly hampered the natural muscular activity of suffering. It is said that the only mercy ever shown to the victim was the offer of a bar of lead to bite on. This modicum of aid apparently helped one to endure the torture of the dreaded cat-o-nine-tails.

The Pain Is Killing Me!

It is little wonder that the violent muscular exertions of extreme pain must be followed by a fatigue that is long and heavy. Torture has sometimes killed its victim by driving beyond the body's capacity to resist and to repair its damage.

In ancient England, part of the penalty for treason was the horrible procedure of drawing and quartering. It began with hanging by the neck, but *not* until the victim was dead. He must then be disembowelled, or drawn, and the entrails must be burned before his eyes. To complete the penalty, his head must be cut off and the body divided into four parts. This was the quartering. Somewhere in this hellish torture, there comes a total collapse of nervous impressions and, with it, a blessed peace.

You were not drawn and quartered, but we did leave you back there with your fingers caught in a machine. Meanwhile, help arrived to extricate you. But you are fatigued from the frantic exertions. Perhaps a sedative is needed to calm your nerves. Let your heavy eyelids droop. Let your eyes stray a little out of focus. You may even let your thoughts wander to the brink of dreams. As you turn to the closing pages of this book, it is safe at last to talk about drowsiness. Just lie back and give in to your exhaustion. What follows will be a shot of verbal morphine.

Ho-Hum

When the body grows fatigued, the respiration grows correspondingly shallow and the circulation sluggish. A dullness and inactivity ensue— the earmarks of *drowsiness*. It is the brain that grows drowsy as a consequence of the depleted flow of blood and the blood's reduced oxygen

content. This state of affairs calls for a reflex that, for a while, brings vigor quickly to the respiratory and circulatory apparatus.

Very possibly you've never heard of a pandiculation, but that is what you indulge in when you stretch and stiffen your trunk and limbs. Dogs and cats are well known for their frequent displays of this mechanism. But you also pandiculate quite well, perhaps the last thing before retiring or the first thing upon rising. Here, then, is a physical exertion that hastens the flow of blood throughout the body and stimulates the chest muscles to deeper breathing.

A comparable mechanism, beginning in the jaw and throat region, is the oscitation, which is just a plain yawn. This amounts to a muscular reflex that causes a deep and vigorous inhalation of air into the lungs and, at the same time, by its activation of throat and chest muscles, further stimulates the flow of blood to the drowsy brain. The first sensation, after opening the mouth into a tall O, is that of a high arching of the soft palate above the back of the tongue. You can watch this in your mirror. Next comes a swelling of the chest as a great draught of air is sucked down quickly into the lungs. The head may even be rocked backward by the rising chest. And there may be a momentary sensation of pressure in the ear canals (Eustachian tubes) such as that set up by sudden changes of altitude in an airplane or elevator. Then comes a violent compression of the chest as air is expelled slowly from the lungs. On this down stage of yawning, you may discover that a fine watery spray from your gaping mouth spatters this very page of print. The spray is saliva squirted during the yawn from very small openings in the mucous membrane under the tip of your tongue. On this account, a swallow is very apt to follow a yawn. Since the yawn is a form of violent expiration, there will be forcible closure of the eyes at the top of the yawn. You may find it amusing to try to keep your eyes open throughout a yawn. The specific details for the closure pattern were given in Chapter Three. It is sufficient to note here that repeated yawning will bring tears to the eyes. But this should be no surprise for those who understand the details of violent expiration.

It is difficult to say why yawning is provoked by suggestion, such as the sight of others yawning. Even concentrating your attention on a big letter O can trip you into yawning. The phenomenon of empathy would seem to be suspect. Probably the muscles of the mouth make an undetectable and subconscious effort to simulate the oval outline of what is seen or imagined. Since the O formation of the mouth is the first link in the chain of reflex movements, probably this acts as a trigger to high

DROWSINESS

HO-HUM

PANDICULATION (STRETCH)
AND
OSCITATION (YAWN)

arching of the soft palate, which in turn triggers the swelling of the chest, and so on.

Incidentally, did you yawn your way through the last paragraph or two? The need to squeeze the eyes shut, not to mention the accumulating moisture in them, may well have interfered with your reading. But this is the end, at last. So close your eyes and let slumber overtake you. Your face deserves a rest.